Reel Rituals

Reel Rituals:
Ritual Occasions from Baptisms to Funerals in Hollywood Films 1945-1995

Parley Ann Boswell

Paul Loukides

Bowling Green State University Popular Press
Bowling Green, OH 43403

Copyright 1999 © Bowling Green State University Popular Press

Library of Congress Cataloging-in-Publication Data
Boswell, Parley Ann.
    Reel rituals : ritual occasions from baptisms to funerals in Hollywood films, 1945-1995 / Parley Ann Boswell, Paul Loukides.
       p.   cm.
    Filmography : p.
    Includes bibliographical references.
    ISBN 0-87972-791-8 (clothbound). -- ISBN 0-87972-792-6 (pbk.)
    1. Rites and ceremonies in motion pictures. I. Loukides, Paul.
II. Title
PN1995.9.R56B67   1999
791.43'655--dc21   99-11699
                                                                  CIP

DISCARDED

DEDICATION

For Kennedy Hutson and Boswell Hutson,
who have made the rituals of my life real.
Parley Ann Boswell

This one too for Nora, Jason, and Cindy
with love and gratitude.
Paul Loukides

CONTENTS

Foreword	ix
Introduction	1
1. The Rituals of the Godfathers	11
2. The Ritual Occasions of Childhood	25
3. Wedding Celebrations	43
4. Wakes, Funerals, and Burials	65
5. Luminous Moments in Hollywood Films	85
Afterword	109
Notes	115
Filmography	123
Works Cited	131
Index	137

ACKNOWLEDGMENTS

I am grateful to Eastern Illinois University for a Faculty Research Grant in 1994 and a sabbatical leave in 1996. I also thank the following people, who have listened and talked to me about movies with ideas, patience, and good humor while I worked on this book: Mary Jane Boswell, Shauna Carey, Linda Coleman, J. J. Gittes, John Guzlowski, Dana Ringuette, Stephen Swords, Craig Titley, and Nancy Workman.

Parley Ann Boswell

FOREWORD

Film conventions, like all cultural conventions, can tell us something about who we are or were in a given historical moment or period. What the best studies of film conventions have shown us is that bodies of films in which there are baseball games or atomic monsters or bimbos or classic Western heroes or Arabs can reveal something about our cultural attitudes and values and the ways they change or remain the same over time. Would the same be true of one of the most common conventional scenes in films, all those funerals and weddings and graduations that Hollywood has presented to us over the decades?

Some film conventions, like pervasive racial stereotyping, have received a good deal of scholarly attention. Other conventions, like meal scenes or geographical stereotyping have, at best, a modest literature. In our initial conversations about the subject of this book, we were struck by the fact that ritual occasions in the movies—weddings, baptisms, funerals, birthday parties and so forth—had not yet generated much scholarly interest even though they were among the most commonplace scenes in popular films. Virtually everyone we talked to about ritual occasions had a favorite movie wedding or funeral or baptism to share. Sometimes those ritual occasions were sweet or poignant moments, such as the wedding in *Best Years of Our Lives*. At other times the rituals were comic disasters such as the weddings in *Private Benjamin* and still others were the occasions of real moral dissonance like the baptism-killing sequence in *The Godfather*.

As we surveyed the obvious and immediate examples that we and our colleagues could generate, we realized that we had a vast number of films to examine—more than could be credibly handled in a journal-length essay. As we looked further, it became a real question as to whether a modest-sized book would be sufficient; there were clearly hundreds, perhaps thousands, of ritual occasions in film from the earliest days of the silents to yesterday's box office hits.

Compounding the problem of overabundance was the fact that nowhere in the large and growing literature on American popular film is there an index that will tell what films have a wedding or a funeral or a birthday party or a baptism or a bar mitzvah or a graduation. As important and as commonplace as ritual occasions are in the movies, the absence of any kind of systematic indexing reinforced the idea that only recently have film scholars begun to recognize the real importance of examining film conventions as reflections of American culture.

What our preliminary survey also confirmed was our suspicion that what we had already thought was true: ritual occasions in the movies are typically stock or formulaic elements which occur without regard to film genres. There are funerals in war films, comedies, musicals, Westerns, costume dramas and gangster films. Weddings appear in melodramas, horror films, action-adventure movies, musicals, sci-fi films and virtually every other genre. Like many other movie conventions, ritual occasions are such versatile and adaptable plot elements that they fit into all genres if not all films.

The wide spread of ritual occasions across film genres and the entire history of film suggested to us that we needed some fundamental guiding principles to limit and focus our study. We recognized that looking for particular film conventions can be a haphazard process in which the dominating principle becomes searching for films that support the writers' thesis, wherever those might be found. In planning this book, we resolved to concentrate on the top forty films of the fifty-year period 1945-1995, and to use our own extensive movie-watching experiences, the help of colleagues, and bibliographic searching to give us the titles of a core of films to be examined.

Once we had viewed several hundred films from our constantly growing must-see list, and felt ready to move beyond the note-taking stage to the preparation of a manuscript, it was necessary to confront the issue of having perhaps—even probably—neglected a number of important films. We did not view all of the two thousand most popular films from 1945 to 1995; indeed we had not reviewed each of the top thousand films. We decided that we would not watch popular films like *Old Yeller* (1957), or *Broken Arrow* (1950) or *Mogambo* (1953), or *The Love Bug* (1969) even if that choice meant we might neglect some significant ritual occasions in very popular films.

Two elements shaped our decision to abandon the goal of being utterly exhaustive and thoroughly systematic. The first was the obvious and terrible math of indexing a thousand or two thousand films. Two to four thousand hours of movie watching translates into one to two years of forty-hour weeks devoted exclusively to watching films. Much as we love movies, we balked at that prospect.

But in fact, it was the second element in our analysis which convinced us that even if we were not going to be the ones to generate a definitive filmography of ritual occasions in the movies, we had seen and found more than enough material to describe patterns we were confident would be present in any unexamined films of the period. It was those patterns, documented in the several hundred films used in this study, that excited us. While we have tried, then, to represent fairly the ritual occasions in America's most popular films from 1945 to 1995, we have not tried to be exhaustive; we have also used earlier films, foreign films which had a significant American audience, and some less-than-popular American films when we believed those films helpfully illuminated the uses of ritual occasions in mainstream American movies.

Among the other limits of this text, we must also acknowledge that there are a number of ritual occasions important to large numbers of people that have not found their way into this book. The coming-out party in either its WASP or Latino variants is not present here, nor is the bris nor any of the native American coming-of-age or initiation rituals. These ritual occasions are, in fact, quite rare in film and that rarity makes the identification of any real pattern problematic if not impossible.

Other, more common ritual-laden occasions like Christmas or Hanukkah or Easter or Ramadan or Memorial Day or the Fourth of July are barely mentioned. Some, like Christmas, deserve a study of their own. Christmas movies are, after all, nearly a genre unto themselves and scores of other films use Christmas as a kind of emotional or thematic backdrop for the film's main action (see *Godfather I & II*). The other holidays that appear in varying frequencies in the movies are, like Christmas, broadly celebrated cultural occasions rather than the personalized or small-group occasions which are the focus of this study. That difference, between the personal and localized and the societal and broadly based, has an important dimension in the movies.

Birthdays, baptisms, funerals, weddings, graduations and bar mitzvahs are, virtually by definition, focused on the individual or the family. They mark and celebrate significant turning points in the lives of individuals and families; they are public ritual occasions of important life changes for the participants and, as we shall see, the significance of any particular ritual celebration is determined by the practitioners. Funerals can become farce; weddings can be tragic; baptisms can celebrate hypocrisy.

National or cultural holidays, on the other hand, may affect individuals or families, but their meaning or significance as ritualized occasions does not depend on or memorialize any contemporary individual performance. Holidays celebrate historical events (even New Year celebrations focus on the moment the new year arrives) and afford participating members an occasion to participate in recognizing the importance of the event without being central to its meaning. The historical event being celebrated does not depend on any small group of individuals for its value. Even if Scrooge should fail to find redemption through the spirit of Christmas, the spirit of Christmas remains inviolate; Thanksgiving dinner can be a disaster (as it often is in the movies), but the national celebration still has meaning.

The focus of this text is solely on those ritual occasions celebrated as marks of important life changes in the individuals who participate. The ritualized events that we have documented and examined suggest that in American movies ritual occasions are typically less than transformative events, but typically more than simple empty ceremonies. The tension between the promise of an authentic ritual occasion and an event devoid of meaning recurs across genres and varieties of ritual occasions in ways which suggest a complex ambiguity toward rituals in both American film and American culture. This book is an attempt to examine that tension and the complexity that arises from it. In our movie weddings, funerals, baptisms, bar mitzvahs, birthday parties and graduations, we recognize and understand transformative events in the lives of movie characters as reflections of American attitudes and values. Ritual occasions in the movies can bring us to laughter and tears and hope and regret; the chords they strike suggest the complex intersection between American movies and our lives.

Paul Loukides
Parley Ann Boswell

INTRODUCTION

In life—or in film—ritual occasions are dramatic performances. When we celebrate the ritual occasions of our families, our friends, or our communities, we are participating in dramatic enactments, complete with our various roles, props, stages, and audiences. The formal occasions of our lives reflect the dramas of our religions, our nationalities, our ages, or our relationships. We celebrate these narratives of our lives with silence, with laughter, with applause, or with tears.

When we participate in the ritual occasions of our own families, faiths, or cultures, we almost always know how these dramas play out. As part of any community, we learn what to expect, and what will be expected of us during a ritual occasion. Rarely do ritualized events hold surprises for us; like the mythologies, folk tales, and parables of our cultures, ritual dramas are narratives already inscribed, and we most often know how they begin and how they end.

Anthropologist Roger D. Abrahams, in his essay "The Language of Festivals," makes the point that although the ritual celebrations of a culture may change through generations and "come to mean something very different," we still rely on "the same vocabularies" of ritual. We use "objects and actions which are heavily layered with cultural and historical meanings," and we "enter into these fantasy times enthusiastically because they continue to offer times out of the ordinary" (163). Indeed, ritual occasions are not ordinary life; they are scenes of fancy and fantasy, sometimes of tragedy. They are drama.

As Americans we spend much time and money documenting the ritual occasions of our personal lives. We take photographs of birthday parties, we videotape weddings and graduations, we display pictures of deceased family members at funerals. Hollywood uses its understanding of these rituals to imitate our lives, and we, in turn, understand these scenes as much more than recreations of familiar events. Movies have the power to offer us ritual occasions like no other medium, and to project our needs and fears through these ritual scenes in complex and profound ways.

In the pluralistic culture of twentieth-century America, the dramas of our ritual occasions—of baptisms, bar mitzvahs, birthday parties, graduations, weddings, and funerals—have been represented and recreated for us repeatedly by that most American of all dream weavers: Hollywood. No other industry, art medium, or institution has paid more lavish attention to the rites and ritual occasions of Americans than the movie industry. For almost one hundred years, American films have taken our most revered rituals and used them in the telling of our stories, reflecting the formalized dramas of our lives back to us on screen after screen. How Hollywood has reflected, represented, and imitated the ritual occasions of the cultures of the United States in the years since World War II is the focus of this study.

* * * * *

A book on ritual occasions in American popular film depends, in part, on the extensive literature about ritual as described by anthropologists, sociologists, and religious philosophers. Among the first passages we encountered was the following: "Has modern man outgrown his need for ritual? Many would argue that he has, that ritual is nothing more than primitive behavior that no longer serves any useful purpose. The authors . . . would disagree" (Lawson 11). That passage suggests some of the fundamental questions being raised by those who have chosen to study the place of ritual in contemporary life. It reflects the concern that in our society, weddings, baptisms, funerals, bar mitzvahs, birthdays, and graduations (the most formal ritual occasions of our culture) have largely been stripped of meaning and/or transcendental purpose.

Victor Turner and many other commentators on ritual define it as "prescribed formal behavior for occasions not given over to technological routine, having reference to beliefs in invisible beings or powers regarded as first and final causes of all effects" (79). Tom F. Driver, in *The Magic of Ritual* says, "The *techne* of ritual, is utterly different from modern technology. Its field of action is not an objectified physical world but a divine, human, animal and vegetative cosmos of mores, moralities, and mutual relationships" (47).

Have the rituals—both major and minor—in our culture and in our films been stripped of any hint of transcendent meaning? Are the most common ritual occasions of our culture largely presented as empty social occasions of no more significance than a cocktail party or a mall opening or a small town parade?

There are many other questions to be addressed before looking at the obvious formal occasions of weddings, baptisms, funerals, graduations, and birthdays. Among the core issues to be resolved is whether there is, indeed, a fundamental difference between formalized or ritualized behavior and those occasions that we can call ritual occasions. On that issue, the literature reflects a deep division.

Erik Erikson argues that once stripped of transcendental meaning, rituals become mere ritualism, which is to say rote or prescribed behavior with no more (and no less) meaning than the formalities of greetings, the prescribed sequences needed to work on a computer, or the rules of a game of cards. "Ritualization," Erikson writes, "is perverted into what could be called pseudo-ritualization, or more simply, ritualism. This takes many forms, from mere compulsive compliance with daily rules to the obsessive-repetitive expression on fanatic and delusional vision" (90).

However, other writers seem to agree with Ray Browne, who writes that:

... despite the fact that some of the rituals have lost their base in religion and mysticism (a large number still have these roots) and become what Erik Erikson in perhaps too fine a distinction calls ritualism because they are empty and meaningless rituals, and although rituals have become modified in intensity and perhaps in the number of true believers, they have perhaps not become any less permeating and influential on individuals and society in general. Rituals stunted and inhibited in one place surface in other places and in other ways since apparently they are necessary to motivate conscious and unconscious actions of individuals. (1)

For writers like Browne, shopping, watching television, and applying makeup can be viewed and understood as rituals.

In the abstract, questions about the difference between true and empty rituals are not particularly interesting. In the concrete world of life and the movies, the questions are central to understanding the ritual dimensions of life in America. We are, after all, a highly formalized society in which everything from getting an education to filing a tax return to booting up a computer or programming a VCR must be done within highly prescribed procedures. Formalized events in American life are legion. Indeed industrialized societies depend on highly structured behavior; without the protocols of formalized behavior tightly structured societies simply cannot function. In so far as the movies reflect our everyday formalized behaviors (the degree to which they do not is an interesting topic in itself) like getting licenses, filling out forms, driving in a lawful manner, lighting a cigarette, or displaying good manners, film cannot escape depicting ritualized behavior. On the other hand, when we distinguish between the merely formalized and those occasions which are recognized as special formal occasions, then weddings and birthdays are sufficiently different from everyday formal behavior to be examined as ritual occasions of a special kind.

The difficulty of equating formal occasions and ritual occasions is that such a definition does not leave room for differentiating between simply formalized events and those events which have, throughout history, been seen as special, transcendent, and transformative not just for the individual but for the family, tribe or group. Even when the social purpose of an event is the same—as in the case of burying the dead—there is a long tradition which insists that a funeral is a genuine ritual occasion that has a dimension of spirituality or transcendence marking it as different from a simply pragmatic disposal of a body. That elusive difference is, for many writers, like Victor Turner and Roger Abrahams, that which separates the merely formal from true ritual.

As we began our examination of some of the many films with formal ritual occasions, it quickly became clear that the distinctions made by Turner, Abrahams, Erickson and others between rituals that retain some sense of transcendence or "luminosity," and ritualized occasions that have been emptied of transcendent or religious significance provided a useful—if inexact—way of distinguishing important differences between the filmic presentations of various ritual occasions. (Note: we have chosen to use the neutral term "ritual occasions" to designate formal social occasions—weddings, baptisms, etc.—which might be real rituals in Turner's sense, or simply ritualized occasions, devoid of transcendent meaning.)

Although transcendence and a spiritual dimension are central to the definition of true ritual which we came to use in this study, like Turner and others, we do not see spirituality and transcendence as necessarily arising out of religious belief or the formalities of various organized religions. In the definition being used here, a ritual is different from a ritualized event or from formalized behaviors precisely because rituals lead to some sense of transcendence, transformative growth or spirituality for both individuals and for social groups. Starting with that nominal definition of rituals as opposed to ritualized occasions, we set out to examine as many weddings, baptisms, funerals and so forth, as we could find among the most popular films of the past fifty years.

* * * * *

A ritual occasion in film is, from the perspective of the audience, both a familiar event and an event fraught with ambiguity and tension. As we observe several times in the text, ritual occasions of any kind are relatively rare as story-ending events. Put another way, ritual occasions like weddings and funerals have not evolved as conventional ways to resolve the tensions of a plot or story; rather, they have earned their place primarily as means of furthering the conflicts of movie plots. In fairy tales and romance novels, the hero and heroine marry and live happily ever after; the story ends with a marriage and the promise of a blessed union. In film, weddings are rarely the last act; their promise is not one of resolution, but of ongoing conflict and development.

Does this pattern suggest that American audiences accept the idea that formal ritual occasions are, by nature, deeply ambiguous in their meaning and effect? Are weddings and the receptions that follow colored by our perceptions and awareness that more than half of all marriages will end in failure? Do we see graduations as hollow and tension-wrought events because we recognize that graduations are not necessarily causes for celebration?

We had initially begun this study with a sense that the ritual occasions in films would, in fact, most often have the kind of special meanings and functions that have traditionally adhered to certain ritual occasions. Historically, weddings, funerals and baptisms were not just about marking an event; a funeral traditionally was both an occasion for grief and a celebration of life. Funerals were occasions for healing and renewal and, in a religious sense, occasions to reaffirm the primacy of the spiritual dimension over the temporal. Weddings, at least in their traditional language, were about the joining of both flesh and soul in the sight of God. A wedding marked one of life's passages; the forsaking of all others, the creation of a new family, an occasion of life's joys to be celebrated with food, drink, music, laughter and tears. Even secular rituals like graduations and birthdays seemed to be more than public displays of awarding diplomas or acknowledging the passage of yet another year. Family and friends came together to witness and celebrate an important passage in the life of the graduate or the birthday celebrant. Baptisms and bar mitzvahs were, after all, about joining a faith and affirming the importance of the spiritual dimension.

Ritual occasions, at least in the abstract, seemed like a place to find transcendence, transformation and spirituality—even in the movies. What we found instead was that ritual occasions in the movies are most often secular events, and often events which do not reconcile or resolve tensions, but rather create dissonance and disorder—the very antithesis of the traditional purposes of rituals.

But while most of the films discussed in this study present us with a movie vision of an America in which formal ritual occasions are presented as ritualized occasions in which transcendence and luminosity are entirely absent, it is also clear that film is capable of reminding us that rituals can be rich in transcendent meaning.

Weddings, which in films are most often simply presented as ritualized occasions (as in 1939's *Gone with the Wind* or 1988's *Working Girl*), can, in a few films, like *The Sound of Music* (1965) and *Fiddler on the Roof* (1971), suggest, if not insist, that we are watching the enactment of a true ritual where more is happening than a prescribed social bonding. Birthdays, which in films are often empty and even destructive occasions—consider the birthday scenes in *East of Eden* (1955), *The Graduate* (1967), *Tootsie* (1982) and *Fame* (1980)—can also, in rare films like *Crimes of the Heart* (1986), suggest a transcendent dimension where love, joy and a sense of magic arise out of the simple rites of a birthday celebration.

Funerals, as we shall see, are very often painfully awkward occasions entirely focused on the living. The funeral of Snowdon in *Catch 22* (1970), for example, is presented as an onerous and empty duty for everyone except the two spectators: Yossiarian, who is seated naked in a tree, and Milo Minderbender, who wants Yossiarian to try chocolate-covered cotton. No healing or understanding comes from this occasion. On the other hand, the funeral in *The Yearling* (1946) presents a time of genuine grief focused on the loss of a child and a sense of growth, healing, and social integration among the mourners.

If formal occasions like the baptism in *The Color Purple* (1985) present us with a sense of the sacred, then the baptisms in *Billy Bathgate* (1991), *Leap of Faith* (1992), and *The Godfather* remind us that even as fundamentally religious a ritual occasion as a baptism (which is, after all, an initiation into a world of faith), can be made profane.

Equally, as secular an occasion as a graduation can be, films like *An Officer and a Gentleman* (1982) remind us that the celebration of a life transition or an initiation can give formal substance to important and transcendent changes in the life of an individual and his social community.

Although some ritual occasions in the movies did, in fact, suggest a transcendent dimension, we became aware that even the best of those moments rarely measured up to the sense of extraordinary event that some films without formal occasions seemed to display. Curiously, the one kind of film that seemed to regularly incorporate all of the dimensions of true ritual occasions as defined by writers like Turner and Abrahams, was the sports film. Films about baseball, football, track, wrestling, boxing, and basketball often not only had a transformative and spiritual dimension for the participants, they also included a genuine dimension of social connection wherein both spectators and participants were brought together in celebration.

In sports films which seem to incorporate the transcendent dimensions of true ritual occasions, it is the final major event of the film that reaches this potential. The last race, the last game, the last match are used to resolve conflict and tension and bring a sense of completion to the struggles preceding that final effort. Unlike weddings, baptisms, funerals, birthdays, or graduations, the major sporting event has a conventional place at the end of the film; it is the place where conflicts will be resolved. Sports films use the formal occasion of the last competition in a way that suggests that they are true ritual occasions. As in fairy tales, the final ritual leads to resolution and growth.

Like all cinema, Hollywood films are never quite what they seem. The very nature of storytelling on film (which looks deceptively simple, but which never is simple) provides multiple perspectives, time frames, and layered narratives which require close attention. Reviewing a series of ritual occasions from Hollywood films will reveal much to us about the institution that is "Hollywood," and about the American society of which Hollywood is a part. A long look at hundreds of Hollywood movies helps reveal both what we are like, and what we *wish* we were like. Our study of rituals, beginning with a close look at the Corleone family in *The Godfather* epic, will allow us to consider how American films, and the American society that consumes and encourages these films, have both shaped and been shaped by the complicated depiction of our rites.

1

THE RITUALS OF THE GODFATHERS

At the end of *The Godfather II,* after burying his mother, killing Hyman Roth, and ordering the murder of his brother Fredo, Michael Corleone (Al Pacino) sits alone silently and remembers. Privy to his memory, we make the journey back with him to his father's home on December 7, 1941, and we see the Corleone children, young adults all, preparing a birthday celebration for their father. We recognize much that is familiar in this scene: the various personalities of the Corleone children, their relationships to each other, the power of their absent father. What we may not recognize as familiar to us in this scene is actually an aspect of the film with which we are so familiar that we probably take it for granted. This memory of Michael's is grounded in a ritual occasion—a birthday celebration.

Like many of the important moments of the *Godfather* trilogy, this flashback of Michael's comes to life for us not just because we understand the Corleone family dynamics or the significance of the dialog, but also because we understand the ritual of the birthday party. There are probably many things about the Corleones that do not make sense to us; by this point in the film, Michael Corleone in particular may seem remote and impenetrable to us. The young man we sympathized with in *The Godfather* has become a moral monster. However, what makes Michael, isolated in his "bunker" in Tahoe, accessible to us is that we can share this one aspect of his life with him: he and his family celebrated their birthdays. We know the Corleones because we share their rituals and their celebrations.

Falling almost exactly in the middle of our 1945-1995 timeline come *The Godfather* (1972), *and The Godfather Part II*

(1974), which include an extensive variety of ritual occasions. With the third *Godfather* film in 1990, this epic trilogy presents nearly every common ritual occasion on our list. The flashback to the Don's birthday party at the end of *Godfather II* is, of course, only one example of how powerful ritual occasions can be to the film. Paying close attention to the many rituals and celebrations in all three *Godfather* movies can certainly give us a format for exploring the value of rituals in other Hollywood films. The *Godfather* films offer a way of reading rituals that becomes a touchstone for study of other Hollywood movies.[1]

Beginning with and including Connie Corleone's wedding celebration in *The Godfather,* there are three weddings, three funerals, four birthday celebrations, one Catholic confirmation, a baptism, two religious street festivals, and two Catholic masses in the entire *Godfather* trilogy. There are also scenes set during the Christmas season, New Year's Eve, and Easter Sunday. Several ritual occasions (like the flashback of the Don's birthday in 1941) coincide with infamous world events. For example, Hyman Roth's sixty-seventh birthday celebration, New Year's Eve, and the Cuban Revolution of 1959 all happen within a short span of time. That Don Corleone's birthday party happens to be the day the Japanese attack Pearl Harbor becomes an important part of Michael's memory, because the Don's birthday celebration and Michael's decision to join the Marines collide during this scene.

The use of rituals and celebrations in the *Godfather* films is extensive and profound, and has often been acknowledged as one of the most powerful aspects of the films by critics and film scholars. "With cinematic élan, the film intercuts religious ceremonies or celebrations with sobering scenes of 'business as usual' . . . . It is a signal motif of the film," write Seth Cagin and Phillip Dray in their study of American films in the 1970s (186-87). Robert B. Ray points out that juxtaposing scenes of celebration with scenes of violent crime is a traditional film technique, and he cites the example of D. W. Griffith's *A Corner of Wheat,* produced in 1909, as perhaps the earliest in a long line of precedents for the *Godfather* films' signature "parallel editing." Juxtaposing, he writes, put the *Godfather* films into this tradition and allowed them to show "that American society functioned on two levels: an ideologically whitewashed exterior and a foundation of predatory violence" (336). The ritual occasions become sites for their own antitheses.

John Yates agrees that these films show the "rottenness" of American business and culture, but that a film about American corruption is "commonplace." "The two movies," Yates writes, "are about American corruption at about the same level as they are about gangsters" (199). What these films are, Yates argues, "are at their deepest level a brilliant revelation of the family, how it worked through the generations . . ." (199). How do these films portray a family? Yates argues that by creating a "real, living, breathing world" in *Godfather I,* Coppola and the actors show us "a family," who, in the "first grand scene of *Part I*," are "engaged in the most familial of rituals, a daughter's wedding" (199). Indeed, using rituals, celebrations, and recognizable traditions of Western culture allows us to understand the unimaginable in these films. Much of what happens in these movies we cannot share with the characters, yet the real, living, breathing world of the Corleones we can see because it comes to us through the series of traditional ritual occasions we share with them.

If *The Godfather* films present us with the story of a family, then Connie's now-famous wedding, as Yates and others have pointed out, is the first of many elaborately choreographed ritual occasions which help introduce that family to us by using a network of symbols and traditions that we already understand from the larger American culture. As will be noted in the chapter devoted to a discussion of wedding scenes in other American movies, Connie's wedding celebration is one of the most important of all American film wedding scenes. Beyond this wedding scene are the many other scenes of ritual and celebration in the *Godfather* trilogy, worth noting because this study of one American family suggests a strategy for evaluating other families and other stories in American movies.[2]

After Connie Corleone's wedding, the next suggestion of a rite or a ritual in *The Godfather* comes when Vito Corleone is shot on the street. We first see Michael and Kay walking in front of Radio City Music Hall, discussing Christmas gifts for the Corleones. Next, we see Luca Brasi dressing to go to his final "meeting," and we see a shot of a store window dressed for Christmas with a Santa and reindeer.

The Don is gunned down on a quiet side street while he is shopping for fruit, his last-minute driver, son Fredo, at the scene with him. Vito's activities appear so innocent (a powerful Don shopping for groceries with his half-witted son) that when he is gunned down, he seems to be a true victim, an unarmed civilian. That the head of the Corleone family, a man who is adept and swift in his judgments and in control of his power, can be seen as a victim here is partly due to the suggestion of the Christmas season. The celebration of the birth of the Christ—an innocent lamb whose story is ultimately one of betrayal and suffering—is a most interesting backdrop for the attack on Vito Corleone. Patrone of a brutal crime family, Corleone looks to be a lamb of God when gunned down during the festive Christmas season.

To avenge his father's shooting, Michael commits a double murder and leaves home to hide in Sicily. The next elaborate scene of a ritual occasion is Michael's wedding to Apollonia. In fact, we follow Michael and Apollonia's ritualized courtship closely. We see them meet, we see him ask her father for permission to court her, we see them walking and talking in the presence of chaperons. Theirs is a graceful, simple wedding celebration followed by the only genuine "love scene" in any of the *Godfather* films.

Michael's beautiful Sicilian wedding serves many functions in the film, not the least of which is to underscore the differences between his new marriage and that of his sister Connie, whose good-for-nothing husband beats her more than once during the film. Michael seems to be an innocent in Sicily; he is renewed by the sacred wedding rituals in his father's pastoral homeland. We begin to see parallels between Vito and Michael Corleone because of the Sicilian wedding scene. As Yates writes, "they [the Sicily scenes] serve as a picture of the world from which

Vito Corleone came, and in which his son Michael operates just as he did. It is a world, existing in the present, that is not too different from the primitive world that spawned the original family" (200). Michael, the college boy and American war hero who has traveled to Sicily to escape retribution for committing murder in America, has been redeemed and rewarded.

There are two final sequences of ritual occasions in *The Godfather,* the funeral of Don Corleone and the baptism of Connie's son Michael. In a scene that is most famous, Don Corleone dies a natural death as he plays "monster" in his garden with his toddler grandson. In the same way the film presents the aftermath of Connie's wedding and not the wedding ceremony itself, it also presents the burial of Don Corleone, and not the funeral. The cortege is massive and elaborate; we see a long procession of limousines and cascades of flowers before we see the grieving family. When we finally do see Michael and his family, we understand enough about the customs of a burial to recognize that this is no ordinary funeral. Michael, Tom, and assorted other dignitaries are doing business, planning meetings, pledging new allegiances in sight of Don Corleone's casket. Before the Don is in the ground, his son has identified a traitor and has planned his next move. And his next move, as he informs Tom Hagen, involves another ritual occasion: "But I'm gonna wait. After the baptism. I've decided to be godfather to Connie's baby. And then I'll meet with Don Barzini. And Tattaglia. All the heads of the five families."

The final ritual sequence of *The Godfather* is undoubtedly the best known sequence of the film. And, unlike the earlier ritual scenes where the audience joins the narrative after the actual public rite has occurred, the baptism scene includes almost the entire rite. This long sequence, a complex example of "parallel editing," combines the baptism of infant Michael Rizzi with the baptism of Michael Corleone as Godfather in stunning ways. Cutting between shots of the infant to shots of Michael's soldiers preparing for battle, or between shots of Michael responding to the priest's question, "Do you renounce Satan?" and shots of brutal, sudden murder, we are stunned into an understanding of the rituals we are watching. Baptism in the Corleone world is by water, fire, and blood.

The visual shots of this sequence and the layered sounds we hear, combine for us the pageantry and sanctity of infant baptism—a ritual which publicly celebrates the innocent soul of the infant—with the violent deaths of five unsuspecting men. We first hear the cry of a baby as we watch a long shot of a cathedral. As Michael approaches the altar and cradles the infant at the baptismal fount, we hear soft organ music appropriate to the ceremony. The priest begins the Latin litany, the organ music grows louder, and we next see a shot of a gun being loaded. As the priest continues the rite, Michael holds the baby's head back. We immediately see a shot of a man in a barber's chair, in the same position as the baby, with his head back and his neck exposed. The music grows ominous.

As the priest prepares to anoint baby Michael Rizzi, Michael Corleone's men prepare themselves by loading guns, dressing in disguises, and getting to the killing site. Back in the cathedral, the organ music crescendos as the priest moves from Latin to English, asking Michael the ritual question, "Do you believe in God, the Father Almighty?" With Michael's assent, the film cuts immediately back to the various murder scenes as Michael's enemies are murdered, one by one, to the strains of loud, dramatic chords from the church organ. Finally, as the priest anoints the infant, the film cuts to shots of dead bodies. The sound track is silent after both the ritual of life and the ritualized murders are completed. The infant baptism has ended at the same time that Michael Corleone's baptism into his new position as Don has begun.

The "signal motif" of these combined sequences at the end of *The Godfather,* according to Cagin and Dray, expresses "a central conflict: the shutting away of Christian ethics in the name of power, revenge, or greed" (187). The sequence functions in many other ways as well. This is Michael's first action as head of the family since his father's death. As revealed by his conversation with Tom at his father's funeral, Michael has planned this first act with the baptism in mind. That he decides to be godfather to his nephew while burying his father so that he can use the opportunity to wipe out his enemies is a devious, brilliant, and cynical maneuver. These two ritual occasions have afforded Michael Corleone the chance to really be a Godfather. By the end of the first *Godfather* film, we understand his position because we understand the rituals (those of his Catholic faith and those of his business) in which he has participated. We have seen him take the sacred vows of a godfather in a Roman Catholic Mass, and in the final shot of the film, we watch him receive a visitor who participates in a ritualized behavior we understand because Michael's father had initiated us to this Family ritual during Connie's wedding: in the same dark room where Vito Corleone did his business, Michael stands with a man who lowers his head and kisses Michael's ring. Michael Corleone is now godfather and Godfather.

Part I concludes with multiple ritual occasions, and *Part II* opens in the same way, with a double ceremonial rite: the funeral of Vito Andolini's father in Corleone, Sicily, and the First Communion of Michael's son Anthony in Nevada. As John Yates points out, the "world of the wedding party in *Part I* is, as is the Tahoe party at the opening of *Part II,* in chaos" (201).

The code by which Vito Corleone ne Andolini lived and built his empire as a young immigrant in New York has begun to change in ways that become clear to the audience because of this communion reception scene. Yates writes:

Frankie Pentangeli stumbles drunkenly through the Tahoe party crowd, an outraged figure from another time, completely lost in a shiny, new world. The waiters call a Ritz cracker with liver "a can of peas," the family in-laws don't understand Italian, and the closest the band can come to the old songs is "Pop Goes the Weasel." (201)

There are other ominous changes. When Michael does business in his office during the party, the tone is decidedly different from the respectful atmosphere of his father's study back in New York. His first guest, Senator Geary, delivers a scathing, ugly declarative to Michael: "I don't like your kind of people. . . . I despise your masquerade—the dishonest way you pose yourself, yourself and your family." Frankie Pentangeli, after waiting "on line" for Michael all afternoon, leaves dissatisfied and without kissing Michael's ring. Michael fights with Connie about her neglect of the family and about her newest boyfriend, whom Michael does not know. In sharp contrast to the security of Connie's wedding celebration inside the safe family enclave in New York in *The Godfather,* Michael's Tahoe compound is not a safe haven for the Corleone family: late in the evening, hit men will shoot at Michael and Kay through their bedroom window.

In one of the final scenes during this long sequence comes one of the most bittersweet moments in the film, when Michael tucks his son Anthony into bed. "Did you like your party?" he asks. Anthony replies, "I got lots of presents. . . . I didn't know the people who gave them to me." His father hesitates, then mumbles "they're friends." We have come to understand Anthony's confusion here. By attending this long First Communion celebration, we have watched Michael Corleone with his "friends," and we now understand that the Corleones do not have "friends." They have "associates," some of whom would like to see them dead. As we watch this first sequence, we understand that the power of the Corleones to function as a cohesive family has deteriorated dramatically since the day when Vito danced with his daughter at her wedding. Michael, a father who struggles to communicate with his son, who treats his sister with hostility and suspicion, also struggles with his power as Don. His Family is in chaos indeed.

The scenes that follow this First Communion party, especially those in which we see public celebrations, parades, or festivals, reveal even more about the role of ritual and the changes in the Corleone empire. When Michael travels to Havana, we see street celebrations, a birthday party for Hyman Roth, and a New Year's Eve party which turns into a national revolution. We are barraged with ceremony and pomp, not unlike Michael, who is nearly overwhelmed in Havana. It is here, amid the bedlam of revolution and New Year's holiday, that Michael barely escapes disaster in many forms. Michael is an astute businessman whose observations about the Cuban rebels lead him to doubt the wisdom of investing in Cuba, and he tries to back out of his deal with Roth. At the same time that his assassination attempt on Roth fails, he discovers the traitor in his family to be his brother Fredo.

The Cuban sequence of *Godfather Part II* is complicated and difficult to follow, and would be even more difficult were it not for the clear signals we get from the ritual occasions imbedded in this sequence. When Hyman Roth cuts his birthday cake, we understand that he is also cutting pieces of his empire to be consumed by the men around him. When the New Year arrives on the dance floor of the Capri Hotel, Michael's is a dance of anguish as he begins the year by embracing Fredo with a kiss of death: "It was you, Fredo, it was you." Against the backdrop of world events and the traditional holiday season, these occasions seem most painful; there is nothing happy about Hyman Roth's birthday celebration, nor about the new year.

The further flashback sequences of young Vito Corleone include scenes of a religious procession (where, in the *Godfather* tradition of astute parallel editing, Vito commits a crime during a holy celebration when he murders Don Fanucci) and a Catholic Mass, where Vito, having just avenged his family by murdering old Don Ciccio, stands proudly with his wife and children on the steps of the cathedral. The world of *Godfather Part II* consistently links murder with Christianity, innocence with brutality, and these flashback sequences help an audience to make the link. By the time we return to Lake Tahoe in 1959, we have a clearer understanding of the relationship of the Corleones to their rituals because of these scenes of rites and celebrations. We have watched Vito Corleone begin his rise as a powerful New York Don by committing murder during a religious celebration, and we have watched his son do the same; we have come to expect that ritual occasions in the world of the Corleones will be defined by this juxtaposition of the sacred and the profane.

The penultimate ritual occasion which appears in *Part II* is Mama Corleone's wake, which is particularly grim. Michael sits alone, his two small children sitting across the room. We are painfully aware that the Corleone men can no longer control their women or their marriages when the story of Mama Corleone's life is juxtaposed to those of Kay, who is now gone, and Connie, who has been estranged from Michael since the first scene of the film.[3] Having seen flashbacks of Vito Corleone's victorious revenge and happiness as a family man in Sicily, we now are faced with Michael's final failure and isolation from his family. He has already indicated to his associate that something will happen to Fredo ("I don't want anything to happen to him while our mother is alive"), so we expect the worst to happen after this funeral scene. Like the funeral of his father in *The Godfather,* we understand that Michael attends to business during this sad moment, by giving a silent order for his brother to be killed. The reconciliation in grief of the two brothers is a sham, a play of Michael's to move Fredo close to him.

And, once again, a ritual occasion helps us to come to grips with this most horrendous deed of Michael's. By the very end of the film, where Michael sits and remembers better days in New York, we have been able to piece his—and his father's—stories together through the help of the family parties, funerals, and religious rituals which have spanned sixty years of their lives. The final scene of the Don's birthday party allows us to feel for the Corleones, especially for Michael, something we would probably not otherwise feel: sympathy. The scene is nostalgic, bittersweet, sad. Michael Corleone, and the world his father created for him, are lost. Michael the college boy who volunteered for military service, has become a man his father would not respect. When Sonny reacts to Michael's news that he has joined the Marines: "Break your father's heart on his birthday," he cannot possibly know how apt his remark is. Michael's actions and decisions since that birthday party on December 7, 1941, have brought him to Lake Tahoe, where he sits alone, having just ordered his own brother's execution. We understand enough about Michael, and enough about Vito, to know that Michael *would* have broken his father's heart.

When *The Godfather Part III* was released in 1990, it opened to great expectations and to mixed reviews. However played when it was first released, one of the aspects of the film which seems consistent with the earlier two films is the use of multiple ritual occasions. We first see Michael receive the Order of Saint Sebastian during a special Mass in 1979, and the sequence includes flashback shots of Michael watching Fredo being executed on Lake Tahoe back in 1959. We watch as the obligatory family photo of the Corleones is taken. Later, we watch Michael's nephew Vincent (Andy Garcia) commit a murder during a religious parade in New York's Little Italy, much of it filmed in parallel shots reminiscent of Vito's murder of Don Fanucci in *Part II*.

We watch Michael and Kay, in Sicily together for their son's operatic debut, as they watch a local wedding party celebrating in the small town of Corleone. We attend a funeral with the Corleone family in Sicily, where Michael attends to business while the funeral rites are underway. And the final sequence of the film includes both a birthday for the treacherous Don Altobello (Eli Wallach) and an Easter Sunday opera performance which suggests both the martyred death of the Christ and shows us the final disintegration of the Corleones in the form of the murder of Michael's daughter, Mary.

If the *Godfather* trilogy is, as Yates has suggested, about a family more than it is a film about the underworld or gangland violence, then we understand the importance of the family by watching these important scenes of ritual occasions. Indeed, *The Godfather* trilogy is a family epic that shows us not so much how empires are created or businesses run, but how families are born, live, and die. We have watched as Vito Corleone built his empire in the 1920s, and we have seen how this empire begins to unravel as Michael tries to negotiate his way through the 1950s. We understand that those characteristics which served the poor immigrant Vito so well—his quick intelligence, his fortitude, his loyalty, his discipline—have, in his privileged American-born son Michael, become dangerous, destructive qualities. By the 1970s, Michael Corleone has made decisions which have destroyed the Corleone family and the empire that his father created.

We are with the Corleones for so many of their traditional rites of passage and celebrations that we know much more about their likes, loves, weaknesses, and fears than we do about their business. As Michael tells his son Anthony in *The Godfather Part III*, "every family has bad memories." We know the Corleones' bad memories because we have seen how they celebrate, grieve, and survive. Through the years of the three movies, we watch them thrive and deteriorate as a family by gauging them against their ritual occasions. It is no accident that *The Godfather III* concludes with a scene of Michael, sick, old, and once again sitting alone, isolated in his own pain, falling over in a chair while a dog wanders around him. We never see a funeral Mass nor a burial scene for Michael Corleone. We have no ritual occasion to mark the demise of the Corleone Family; the Family no longer exists.

To review the *Godfather* films for their scenes of ritual occasions is to acknowledge one of the most powerful displays and uses of ritual in American film. Virtually all of the ritual scenes in these films are common ones to American audiences because they represent basic rites of Western culture. All of them have their counterparts in the world outside of the *Godfather* films, of course. How we behave in groups, how we celebrate or mourn, marry or pray, are rites that Hollywood films have duplicated, distorted, or projected for almost a century. The customs in our culture which these films reflect vary in terms of time, or ethnicity and race, or economic class, yet they share characteristics and patterns. Identifying some basic patterns of the Western festivals and rituals identified in *The Godfather* helps us understand that ritual occasions in Hollywood films most often gain their power from the dramatic conflict between the transcendent promise of the ritual itself and the hard reality of the world where people act out the iron necessities of their lives.

There are, according to anthropologist Roger Abrahams, festivals and rituals.[4] Festivals, including the religious festival, the county fair, the civic parade, have their roots in seasonal celebrations. And in twentieth-century America, although these festivals "have become detached from our work," they still reflect "celebrations of the capacity of increase of the earth . . . by acknowledging the powers of nature and the place of humankind in enhancing that process . . ." (163). Festivals are public, communal affairs which may bring many different and often conflicting needs of the community together. Festivals, Abrahams writes,

> initiate their own energies even while they organize the celebrants for mutual fun and profit. Thus, festivals begin with a bang, literally, with loud noises produced by drums, guns, firecrackers. . . . The vocabulary of festival is the language of extreme experiences through contrasts—contrasts between everyday life and these high times. . . . (167)

The festivals we watch in the *Godfather* films are certainly studies in contrasts between everyday life and something else; they represent, in Abrahams' words, "special renderings of the exchange system of the community" (168). Festivals celebrate abundance and growth, and it is no accident that dollar bills adorn the statue of the Virgin in *Godfather II* or that Vito Corleone improves his economic status after this festival. The public festival scenes in all three films, from Michael's first wedding parade in Sicily, to the parade in Vincent Mancini's Little Italy, serve to help audiences recognize change and growth in the public lives of the Corleone family.

Festivals respond to the calendar year, and we can plan our celebrations (or our murders) accordingly. Rituals, however, respond to birth and death in ways that we cannot always plan. Although they are most often public affairs which share characteristics with festivals, rituals have to do with choices we make in our private lives. They are "responses to the crises of the transitional events of life" in which "the usual passage of time is stopped and the larger life-rhythms are invoked as a means of measuring our days" (167). Abrahams writes:

> . . . when a ritual is celebrated at a point of life-transition, like a death or a marriage, the energies of the celebrants are already raised; the ritual, at that point, simply provides a focus for those energies, and a

vocabulary of significant objects and actions which detail what the occasion means. . . . (167)

"Ritual," he continues, "provides an organizing set of principles, traditional ways of momentarily binding the opposing forces within the community and tying together the past with the present" (167). Certainly, that Don Corleone's rivals all attend his daughter's wedding, that they all come to pay their respects to his family at his funeral, and that the neighborhood bully shows up to dance at Michael's Insignia reception are aspects of ritual in the *Godfather* movies that become very significant details to our understanding of the world of the Corleones. The family ritual becomes the Family Ritual in these films, and becomes our most valuable guide as we explore changes in the world of the Corleones.

According to ritual scholar Ronald Grimes, rituals, like the beings who employ them, are always changing. There are, he writes, certain patterns common to all rituals, but rituals are always evolving to reflect the changes in the group who engages in them. As our rituals evolve, they influence every aspect of the society of which they are a part, and they become part of the "framework" of the society. Rituals, writes Grimes, "are not only embedded in social processes, they also process actors, things, spaces, and times . . . they are in process; they develop and decline" (274). *The Godfather* is a powerful example of how ritual occasions show us the process, development, and decline of a group. From the promise and sunshine of Connie Corleone's wedding, through the unspeakably tragic Easter Sunday that concludes the trilogy, we watch the rise and fall of the Corleones as they move back and forth between the sacred and the profane.

2

THE RITUAL OCCASIONS OF CHILDHOOD

The ritual occasions of American culture—and their changes—are nowhere more clearly presented to us than in this most American of institutions, the movies. We can catch our own reflections by watching how Hollywood has chosen to show us celebrating, communing, or grieving through the years. *The Godfather* trilogy offers us one way of gauging our rituals. Another way, equally challenging and entertaining, is to explore the ways Hollywood has portrayed rituals—from birth to death—in specific scenes of ritual occasions in the movies. By reviewing ritual occasions in the movies, we will also learn about the culture that has produced these Hollywood films, and about the changing needs and values of an American audience that has responded to these movies. We begin where our lives begin: with the ritual occasions of childhood.

In her essay on rites of passage, anthropologist Barbara Myerhoff reminds us of the history of childhood and adolescence in Western culture by explaining that before the Renaissance children were regarded as small adults "without special needs or privileges" (110). The "teenager," also a term associated with Western culture, was "established as a distinctive phase in the human life cycle in America . . . in 1904," and has become such an entrenched aspect of our life cycles that "we quite forget there was ever a time when people passed from childhood to adulthood without being 'teenagers'" (110).[1]

Myerhoff explains that because there are still cultures in the world where there are no adolescent rites to mark these passages, we must acknowledge that celebrating rites of passage associated with this time of life—childhood and adolescence—is not biologically mandated, but is a cultural phenomenon. We are struck with a paradox about the nature of rites of passage, then. Although we call the now-familiar rites of adolescence "natural," they are not necessarily natural, but cultural. As Myerhoff writes, "we belong as much to culture as much as to nature" (110). In other words, we have invented the childhood and teenage years.

Perhaps not coincidentally, the movie industry in the United States was born about the same time as doctors and scholars began using the term "adolescence" to describe the years between childhood and adulthood. It is certainly not a coincidence that as American society has paid more and more attention to (and money on) the culture of childhood and adolescence in the twentieth century, Hollywood films have reflected and projected the rites of passage associated with childhood and beyond with increasing frequency. There may be no better way to explore the American ideal of childhood than to see how Hollywood has presented rites of passage—and the accompanying ritual occasions—through the years.

Until the Andy Hardy films of the late 1930s and early 1940s, there were few American films in which children played significant roles or carried the picture. A major exception, *The Kid* (1921), was truly exceptional; not only was the film named for the child, but it stands today as an American classic about a little child and a little tramp. There were a few others: Joan Crawford's silent films, including *Our Dancing Daughters* (1928), and the 1935 production of *Ah, Wilderness* dealt with the trials of adolescence. There were also the many films of Shirley Temple during the 1930s, which prompted the Hollywood Film Academy to add a new award category, that of Most Promising Juvenile Performer. The second of these awards was presented to Judy Garland in 1939 for her portrayal of perhaps the most famous of all adolescents in American film history, Dorothy Gale in *The Wizard of Oz*.

As more and more children and teenagers became vital members of American society during the years of World War II, Hollywood films began to deal directly with their stories, with protagonists who are struggling to grow up. Only then do we find films which feature genuine Hollywood teenage stars, among them Mickey Rooney, Judy Garland, Deanna Durbin, and Elizabeth Taylor. For the first time, Hollywood productions used children and teenagers to act as more than props, comic relief, or sidekicks, and to celebrate their own rituals—their religious rites of passage, their birthdays, and their graduations.

In 1945, teenager Peggy Ann Garner won the fifth Oscar given in the category of Most Promising Juvenile Performer for her work in a pivotal film about rites of passage, *A Tree Grows in Brooklyn*. In many ways, her portrayal of Francie Nolan marks the beginning of Hollywood's recognition of children and teenagers as people whose stories might be taken seriously on film. *A Tree Grows in Brooklyn* reflects this recognition by showing us significant scenes of Francie's coming of age. The sequences that suggest ritual occasions allow us to recognize Francie's change from little girl to adolescent, and also allow us to view and judge her seriously.[2]

And there *are* many suggestions of ritual occasions in this movie. In fact, rituals and rites are suggested to us during our introductions to most of the adult characters. Early in the movie, Francie's mother Katie (Dorothy McGuire), overworked and humorless, pays the "funeral insurance" out of her meager earnings as a cleaning woman. The first time we meet Francie's Aunt Sissy (Joan Blondell), she talks about her series of husbands, her divorces, and her new marriage to "Bill." Francie's father, dreamer and alcoholic Johnny Nolan (James Dunn), the erstwhile singing waiter, arrives home from his most recent gig, waiting tables at a wedding. In the first scene between him and Francie, he describes to Francie the glittering bride, the champagne, and the flowers; he has brought home leftover food for his family, who celebrate by having a "wedding party" of their own, complete with Katie's wearing of her "wedding combs."

This is really Francie's story, and as the film narrative follows her through several months of life in tenement Brooklyn, we realize that the Nolan family, strapped for money and struggling with Papa's alcoholism, rarely has moments when they are carefree and happy. The scenes in which we see them truly celebrating are vivid: Francie and her brother Neeley (Ted Donaldson) participate in an urban street rite where they win a Christmas tree, and the family celebrates together, singing "Silent Night" while they decorate the tree. When Johnny Nolan dies looking for work, his family gathers for a funeral where Katie is overwhelmed by "how many people loved Johnny." And, in the final ritual scene of the film, Francie, grieving for her dead father, graduates from school in triumph.

Francie's moment of illumination comes just before the graduation ceremony, when she finds a corsage of flowers on her school desk. Her Aunt Sissy watches as Francie reads the card: the flowers are a graduation gift from her deceased Papa, who, according to Aunt Sissy, had left money in her safekeeping months earlier to ensure that Francie would have flowers. When Francie realizes the significance of her father's gesture, she can finally cry for her lost father.

Until this scene, Francie has controlled her grief, her pain, and her anger toward both her parents. She has endured much for a young girl: she has been to her father's funeral and she has helped her mother through childbirth. This posthumous gift from her father could not have come at a more poignant time for Francie, because it was her father who insisted she attend the school from which she is graduating.

This private schoolroom sequence between Francie and Aunt Sissy allows the audience to watch as Francie moves from childish resentment to adult sorrow and understanding. This sequence is followed immediately by a scene of her public graduation, which helps us recognize that she graduates not just from the eighth grade, but from childhood into adulthood. The public ritual of graduation confirms for us that Francie has become wiser and more mature. The ritual has integrity and substance; it is a luminescent moment in which harmony is restored and spiritual growth achieved.

In American movies, the public rituals of childhood—especially scenes of birthday parties, baptisms, and graduations—

most often have more to do with the adults around them than with the children themselves. Like *The Godfather* films, movies often include scenes of infant baptism and religious coming of age to further plot lines in the adult world: *Once Around* (1991), *Last Exit to Brooklyn* (1989), and *Crimes and Misdemeanors* (1989) all include such scenes where very small children's rituals are segues to further the action or to explain adult behavior to us. However, scenes of juvenile birthday parties and graduations often help us recognize characteristics of the children themselves. Francie Nolan's graduation is a good example of how important ritual scenes of graduation can be; since *A Tree Grows in Brooklyn,* there have been other such significant graduations and birthday parties.

The 1950 production of *Our Very Own* begins with the eighteenth birthday of Gail (Ann Blyth). During her birthday party, her younger sister loses her temper and blurts out that Gail is an adopted child. Gail is devastated; much of the film deals with her attempts to understand her relationship to her natural mother (whom she meets) and her adopted family.

To complicate the plot further, we learn that Gail's birthday coincides almost to the day with her graduation from high school, and that she is to be her class valedictorian. Several times in the film, Gail's parents remind her that she has yet to write her speech, but her attempts at writing are frustrating and fruitless to her because she is preoccupied with her status as adopted daughter. The birthday rite of passage conflicts with the graduation to come.

Like Francie Nolan, Gail comes to a new understanding of herself and her family in a scene just before her graduation. As she and her best friend Zaza dress for the occasion, they have a conversation in which Zaza tells Gail that she will have no family at their graduation. Zaza, raised as an only child by an absentee father, reminds Gail that she, Zaza, has no loving family because her mother died when she was born. Gail is visibly shaken during this scene; we can almost see the light bulb come on over her head as she realizes how much she is loved by her adoptive family.

The graduation sequence in *Our Very Own* is the final sequence in the film. We watch Gail's proud family in the audience as they search for her and we watch Gail march to the high school gymnasium stage looking for her family. We hear her speech, a speech she has generated out of her newfound understanding of "family." Although her speech deals nominally with "American citizenship," the subtext is, of course, her recognition of her place as legitimate in her adopted family. We, and her family sitting in the high school audience, can read her code clearly. Gail has not only graduated, she has grown up. Graduation signals yet again a legitimate and profound social rite of real human growth.

Our Very Own was not a highly acclaimed Hollywood production, nor does it remain much more than a curious melodramatic post-World War II drama about the importance of family. In American movies produced after 1945, showing the birthday parties and graduations of teenagers was a projection from Hollywood of national unity and regeneration. Post-war films about teenagers—from these dramas and melodramas to musicals like *A Date with Judy* (1948) and the 1947 version of *Good News*—represented Hollywood's versions of celebration of the home front, and a strongly nostalgic commitment to the family. Ritual occasions in these films are most often treated as real celebrations of important rites of passage.

Our Very Own also demonstrates a very significant characteristic of ritual occasions in American movies, those not just of children but also of adults. As we have seen in *The Godfather* films and others in our study so far, scenes of ritual occasions often bode ill for the characters involved. Gail's birthday party, for instance, becomes not her celebration but her nightmare. What distinguishes the graduation scene in this film, and in *A Tree Grows in Brooklyn,* is that the conflict created by earlier ritual occasions—a funeral for Francie, a birthday party for Gail—is reconciled by the ritual occasions of their graduations at the conclusions of the films. These triumphant graduations reflect a Hollywood trend during the middle decades of the century to use graduations as ritual occasions which truly signify approval, accomplishment, growth, and a sense of community. Often these scenes are concluding scenes, the most dramatic being the musical graduation in *Carousel* (1956), where the graduate's dead father (Gordon McCrea) gets to sing "You'll Never Walk Alone" with his graduating daughter and her mother (Shirley Jones).

Hollywood's reverence and nostalgia for the days of childhood, and for satisfying ritual occasions for children, begin to change gradually during the 1950s with such films as *Rebel without a Cause* (1955) and *The Wild One* (1954). Although neither of these movies includes scenes of ritual occasions, another coming-of-age film produced in 1954, *East of Eden,* includes a significant ritual occasion—a birthday party—which becomes a site not for a sense of maturity and accomplishment for the juvenile characters, but for their loss of innocence and a new sense of understanding of the painful realities of life.

Cal's (James Dean) relationship with his father Adam (Raymond Massey) has always been strained. Yet Cal has worked hard to arrange a surprise birthday party for his father, during which he plans to present him with the gift of a large sum of money Cal has raised by speculating on beans. The party begins pleasantly. Adam, delighted to have his birthday remembered by his younger son, is particularly happy when his older son Aaron (Richard Davalos) announces his own surprise: he and his girlfriend Abra (Julie Harris) are engaged.

Aaron's impromptu announcement is our first clue of the disasters to come during this birthday party. Overshadowed and upstaged by his older, more favored brother's announcement, Cal finally manages to give his father his gift of a large sum of cash. When Cal explains how he made the money, Adam becomes righteously distressed, promptly ordering Cal to "give it back" because his conscience will not allow him to "take a profit from the war." "If you want to give me a present," Adam lectures to Cal, "give me a good life." Cal is devastated by his father's rejection. Sobbing, he leaves the house.

This surprise birthday party will lead to a chain of disasters, and, by the end of the evening (and the end of the film), the lives of all the characters will have been disrupted. Cal delivers his own surprise to Aaron by introducing him to their mother (Jo Van Fleet), a successful madame, whom Aaron has always thought was dead. When their mother realizes that Cal has used her to hurt Aaron, she collapses. By the end of the evening, a distraught Aaron has quickly volunteered for the army and leaves town on a train with the troops. In shock and despair, the boys' father suffers a debilitating stroke as his older son's train pulls out.

The party designed to lead to celebration and reconciliation has turned into a night of unrelieved suffering that cripples the family in *East of Eden*. This disastrous birthday party references other scenes in later Hollywood movies where birthday celebrations become sad or embarrassing affairs for children and teenagers.[3] In *Giant* (1956) we watch a very painful—and embarrassing—birthday party for four-year-old twins Jordie and Julie Benedict, children of rancher Jordan Benedict (Rock Hudson) and his wife Leslie (Elizabeth Taylor). At what looks to be a happy occasion on the front porch of their Texas mansion, Jordan displays an ill temper and stubborn pride which his guests, his wife, and the audience all endure. During the celebration, Jordan forces his crying, frightened son to ride his new birthday pony, stubbornly rejecting Leslie's pleas to take the little boy off the horse. "He's a Benedict," Jordan tells her, "He's going to stay on that saddle if I have to tie him on to keep him there."

Leslie takes the boy off the horse, and Jordie begins to play with his other toys. When Jordan sees the young Mexican farmhand, about the same age as his son, riding the pony easily, he becomes angry. Tearing Jordie away from his toys, Jordan forces the terrified child to ride with him around the yard. This birthday celebration has brought out an ugly arrogance in Jordan that Leslie cannot abide. Shortly after this scene, we see her and her children on a train, abandoning Texas and Jordan, to go back East. It is the birthday party—a ritual occasion that should celebrate family—that instead becomes the catalyst for disruption in the Benedict family. It is also this birthday party that foreshadows the relationship between Jordan and his son Jordie who, as a young man in later scenes in the movie, will reject his father's ranch life to become a physician.

Scenes of ritual occasions in Hollywood movies that involve rebellious or misunderstood children clashing with their parents become increasingly apparent in American films produced after the 1950s. There are significant shifts in the projections of children's rituals in Hollywood films of the 1960s. Not surprisingly, as many other aspects of American culture begin to change quickly during these years, attitudes toward rites, rituals, and toward childhood itself begin to look different in Hollywood films. In 1966, *Who's Afraid of Virginia Woolf?* includes a cruel game between dueling drunks George and Martha, involving an imaginary birthday party for their imaginary son. One year later, *The Graduate,* a movie in which Benjamin's graduation precedes the action of the film, seemed to mark the end of the era of the innocent childhood ritual in Hollywood films, and privileges the themes of generational conflict, disillusionment with the status quo, and aimlessness.[4]

That Benjamin Braddock has already graduated, and that we do not watch this ritual occasion, is significant. What we watch instead of a graduation ceremony are scenes of two parties given in Benjamin's honor. We attend these parties predominantly from Benjamin's perspective. At the first party, a graduation bash hosted by Benjamin's parents, we watch as Benjamin endures a difficult evening. None of the guests seem to be Benjamin's contemporaries; none are his friends. We escape this party with Benjamin when he drives home Mrs. Robinson, the wife of his father's law partner, and we are with him for the rest of the evening as Mrs. Robinson stuns him by propositioning him in her daughter Elaine's bedroom.

The next scene shows us another uncomfortable celebration at Benjamin's home, where his parents are now hosting a twenty-first birthday cookout for him. His father introduces an absent Benjamin as a "feature attraction." In his long, silly introduction, he announces to the waiting guests that he has spent "over two hundred bucks" on Benjamin's birthday gift. Benjamin reluctantly emerges from the house in a wet suit, complete with oxygen tank, and he waddles across the patio toward the swimming pool. From that point, we are in the wet suit with Benjamin, isolated and uncomfortable, as he escapes his parents, their guests, and his party by jumping into the pool and sinking to the bottom. Our last shot in this scene is of Benjamin standing in silence at the bottom of the pool, having escaped his ridiculous party, leaving the celebrating to those above.

These two ritual occasions in *The Graduate* point out a quite different use of ritual occasions than we have seen in earlier Hollywood films. In contrast to scenes of reconciliation or relief, there is no relief in these scenes, only dissonance and conflict. We never get the sense that Benjamin has grown because of these occasions. In fact, we understand that both of these parties represent endings for Benjamin, not beginnings. *The Graduate* uses ritual occasions to highlight alienation by confronting us with multiple layers of unrelieved bad parties where Benjamin is always out of place. These scenes offer us a sense of futility and unreconciled conflict.

Coming out of Hollywood at a time when graduations are usually concluding scenes of fulfillment and pride, and birthdays offer us at least the suggestion of reconciliation or growth, this absence of a graduation and the two bad parties force us into unfamiliar territory in an American film. *The Graduate* suggests that ritual occasions (including the interrupted wedding at the end of the movie) are no longer sacred in Hollywood. Indeed, Benjamin's journey after he returns home, fully graduated with honors, becomes the audience's journey as well. *The Graduate* forces us all to reevaluate the rituals and cultural norms of moneyed American society as Benjamin wanders through postgraduation aimless and disillusioned.

In *Hollywood Films of the 1970s,* Cagin and Dray describe the locus of *The Graduate*:

The Graduate locates the sixties concern for the fragmenting of the family at its extreme geographical and cultural terminus: the affluent suburbs of Los Angeles. The film's premise—that even a "good" young American of the 1960s, one whose behavior is not openly rebellious or outrageous, will stop short of fulfilling his parents' expectations and will in fact begin to suffocate in the family environment—is an essential sixties theme. (30)

Certainly there are many other films of this period, including those discussed by Cagin and Dray, which indicate generational shifts and focus in Hollywood films. *Bonnie and Clyde* (1967), *Dr. Strangelove* (1964), *2001: A Space Odyssey* (1968), and *Easy Rider* (1969) can all be considered American films which project changing values in American society, and point to changes in movie techniques and production standards as well. What makes *The Graduate* such an important title on this list of breakthrough films is its use of American ritual occasions as touchstones for the state of the American family and institutions.

Benjamin's absent graduation, his uncomfortable birthday celebration, and Elaine Robinson's interrupted wedding represent the most clear examples of Hollywood's changing perspective on American rites of passage and ritual occasions. When we watch the film, we understand that graduating from college—even an Ivy League college—guarantees little happiness for the graduate. We see marriages in various states of atrophy, decay, and betrayal. Diplomas mean little in *The Graduate;* wedding vows mean less.

With *The Graduate,* Hollywood's age of innocence concludes. From the late 1960s on, the children and teenagers we see on screen survive rites of passage and ritual occasions that suggest adult situations, problems, and attitudes. The films of the 1970s, '80s, and '90s that include children's rites of passage and rituals reflect a distinct change from earlier Hollywood films with young characters. The sense of triumph and accomplishment that seems to be part of an earlier Hollywood formula for a youth-centered film has been replaced with a sense of angst, anger, or loss. If we look to their rituals, we see that the world is often a sad, treacherous, and empty one for youngsters in Hollywood films of the '70s, '80s, and into the '90s.

Children are often victims in movies of this time, and their lives seem fraught with adult misery. Billy Kramer (Justin Henry) feels as if he is to blame for his parents' breakup through most of *Kramer vs. Kramer* (1979). Iris (Jodie Foster), thirteen-year-old prostitute, has had no childhood in *Taxi Driver* (1976), nor has eleven-year-old prostitute Violet (Brooke Shields) in *Pretty Baby* (1978). Conrad spends most of his time during *Ordinary People* (1980) trying to come to terms with his guilt over his brother's drowning and his own suicide attempt. The list of children with serious, adult-size problems is a long one; Hollywood's youngest characters during the last twenty-five years have been perhaps the saddest and most poignant group of characters to be created by the film community.[5]

Again, if we look to their rituals, we can confirm this. There are few happy birthday parties for young characters during these years, but there are many difficult birthday parties. In *Mommie Dearest* (1981), Christina Crawford spills cake on her birthday dress at her lavish celebration, and her mother Joan Crawford (Faye Dunaway) humiliates her and banishes her from her own birthday party. Ben (Michael O'Keefe) gets drunk with his bullying father Bull Meecham (Robert Duvall) on his eighteenth birthday in *The Great Santini* (1979), and passes out before he can celebrate with the rest of his family, who stand in stunned disbelief as Bull carries Ben into the house. Samantha (Molly Ringwald) spends the whole of her sixteenth birthday in *Sixteen Candles* (1984) trying to understand why no one in her family has remembered to wish her "happy birthday" because of her older sister's impending wedding day; "This is the single worst day of my entire life," she whines to a friend. And in *What's Eating Gilbert Grape?* (1993), Gilbert (Johnny Depp) and his sisters work hard throughout the film to provide their youngest mentally handicapped sibling, mildly retarded Arnie (Leonardo diCaprio), with an eighteenth birthday party, only to have the big day end with their mother's death and the destruction of their home.[6]

Graduations fare no better in recent Hollywood films. There are concluding scenes of triumphant graduations, for instance in

Made in America (1993), *With Honors* (1994), and *Fame* (1980), a film which ends with a delightful explosion of music, dancing, and sheer celebration, but these graduations are not the norm. The joyful rites of passage in these films stand in stark contrast to most film graduations. When imbedded in films, however, significant scenes of graduation do not represent especially happy or rewarding ceremonies for the children involved.

Halfway through *The Last Picture Show* (1971), the main characters Jacy (Cybill Shepard), Duane (Jeff Bridges), and Sonny (Timothy Bottoms) graduate from high school. As the small class sings "Texas, Our Texas" to the accompaniment of a poor pianist, we watch as the camera pans from one face to the next. We recognize Sonny, Jacy, and Duane among the few graduates, and we see that Duane is not paying attention at all. His face is turned toward Jacy, and he is desperately trying to talk to her. We know enough about the characters by this point to understand that high school graduation means much less to Duane than courting Jacy does, and this short scene helps us determine his priorities quickly and effectively. For the young people in the film, a graduation is simply another formal obligation imposed on their lives; it is a ceremony stripped of meaning, a social gathering less meaningful (because more constrained) than going to the movies.

The short graduation scene in *The Last Picture Show* falls almost exactly in the middle of the film, which is rare for a scene of graduation. When graduation scenes show up anywhere in the films besides the conclusions, they are especially valuable to the audience. In the beginnings of movies (*The Group* in 1966, *In Country* in 1989, *Reality Bites* in 1994), they often introduce characters or establish relationships among characters. When they appear, as in *The Last Picture Show,* in the middle of a film, they become a way for us to understand complexities of the film in ways we might not otherwise have understood. The 1993 production of *King of the Hill* is a fine example of how valuable a scene of graduation can be.

In *King of the Hill,* Aaron Kirlander (Jesse Bradford) has much in common with Francie Nolan in *A Tree Grows in Brook-*

lyn. He is poor, living often alone in a shabby hotel in Depression-era Saint Louis (his mother is in a sanitarium; his father is a traveling salesman). Also like Francie, he has forged the necessary papers to allow him to attend a good school outside of his own district. As we get to know Aaron, we admire his fortitude and his ability to survive the poverty and cruelty around him. Also as we get to know him, we feel more and more sympathy for this good-hearted young boy struggling on his own. Nowhere in the film do we feel more compassion for Aaron than during the sequence of his graduation from the eighth grade.

Because he is living alone and by his wits, Aaron must invent ways to accommodate the traditional aspects of graduation without money or family. His graduation is a study in survival: with the help of his only friend, a street-wise teenager who also lives in the hotel, Aaron "borrows" a suit of clothes from the hotel storeroom, tailors it with a stapler, and shows up at his graduation ceremony alone, but in style.

Because Aaron has no family to watch him graduate, when he walks across the stage, and when he wins the "Dewey Achievement Award," the only applause is a loud whistle from his friend, who has sneaked into the back of the auditorium. Aaron trips as he approaches the podium, and seems genuinely uncomfortable when his principal announces that his prize is being awarded for "scholarship and citizenship."

Later, at a rich classmate's reception for the class of 1933, Aaron becomes uncomfortable once again when he tells a series of wild lies about where his parents are. He becomes so uncomfortable, in fact, that he leaves the party by a window, and returns to his fleabag hotel. As the young elevator operator takes him up to his flat, she comments about his graduation, and gives Aaron his only graduation gift: a pack of gum.

From this sequence, we understand much about Aaron. He is a careful and deliberate thinker, who sustains himself by just barely staying within societal boundaries in order to survive. Lying and stealing (or borrowing) are part of Aaron's code of honor because they hurt no one, but they allow Aaron access to knowledge and privilege otherwise denied him by his economic circumstances. From this graduation scene, we learn that to a young man whose life is defined by poverty and loneliness, graduating from eighth grade does not mean much; the ceremony is, in fact, a problem, not a celebratory moment in his life. We understand from this sequence that thirteen-year-old Aaron Kirlander has a maturity well beyond his years because it is necessary, and that he knows that coping with a silly eighth-grade graduation is not the most difficult problem he will face.

Although *King of the Hill* takes place in 1933, it was produced in 1993, and reflects the realistic, often cynical Hollywood graduations of the 1990s, not the nostalgic ones of the 1930s. The graduation ceremony in this film shares more with *The Graduate* than it does with *Ah, Wilderness,* a film made in the 1930s, in which a teenage protagonist graduates from high school. When young Richard (Eric Linden) graduates, his family attends the ceremony, and listens to his passionate valedictory speech. Although his father disapproves of the speech (Richard condemns the "capitalist" society which produces "wage slaves" in his speech), he still beams with pride when Richard collects his diploma. The family goes home and celebrates together, and we get a real sense of community and love. For Aaron in *King of the Hill,* that kind of meaningful ceremony and celebration are only stories he can imagine; he understands that winning a medal or attending a graduation party are not especially significant.[7]

Graduation ceremonies increasingly reflect the attitude toward ceremony that Aaron seems to have: ceremonies are superfluous and often suggest crisis. No longer are children's ritual occasions moments of sentimentality or nostalgia—Aaron's story is never a nostalgic look at poverty or desperation, but a realistic and sometimes grim acknowledgment of injustice in childhood. When we most feel for Aaron—when he graduates and celebrates without much attention—we feel for him not because he is poor, but because he is a child.

From the missing graduation in *The Graduate,* to the pathetic one in *The Last Picture Show,* to Aaron's poignant one, we see that Hollywood has increasingly come to portray graduations as it does birthday parties: as annoyances and empty rituals that suggest the hollowness and wastefulness of a world of adults. In Hollywood, stories on film about children are usually intended to be viewed by adults, and American audiences have come to expect that children's rituals will signal trouble or sorrow, often at the children's expense. For example, the graduation scene in *I Know Why the Caged Bird Sings* (1979) suggests the profound racism confronting the grade school graduates. When valedictorian Marguerite (Constance Good) leads her class in the singing of the Negro National Anthem, "Lift Ev'ry Voice and Sing," the white administrators sitting on the podium are angry and threatened. In the opening graduation scene of *In Country* (1989), we learn that high school graduate Samantha's (Emily Lloyd) father died in Vietnam before she was born, and that she does not live with her mother, but lives instead in near-poverty conditions with her disabled uncle (Bruce Willis). For her, graduation means little; her life is a constant struggle to make ends meet and care for her uncle. The first scenes of *Reality Bites* (1994) represent emptiness and cynicism among the college graduates. The class valedictorian, Leila (Wynona Rider), announces in her speech that she knows that "the answer" to life is "nothing," and receives loud applause from her peers. Another character, in cap and gown, proclaims that her social security number was "the only thing I learned in college." These are not happy occasions nor happy, fulfilled graduates. Hollywood shows us juvenile ritual occasions that project cynicism, disappointment, and isolation. Like Benjamin Braddock's two parties in *The Graduate,* such films suggest endings but not beginnings.

Children's parties in adult films have come to function as sites where we see vulgarity, hypocrisy, and crisis. In *Steel Magnolias* (1989), we watch a family birthday party for a one-year-old boy. Although the family seems to be celebrating, we have been told earlier that this baby's mother (Julia Roberts) is a diabetic who has compromised her health profoundly by giving birth. For us, and for the adults at this baby's birthday party, the joy is tinged with worry and sorrow. In *Fame,* when Doris (Maureen Teefy), an aspiring drama student and performer, is forced by her bullying, manipulative mother to sing "Happy Birthday" to a group of crying, whining toddlers at a large birthday gathering of people Doris barely knows, she is humiliated. Nothing about this birthday celebration seems joyful or rewarding to Doris or to the audience. Instead it looks vulgar and wasteful, bringing clearly into focus for us the problems between Doris and her mother. Children's ritual occasions have been co-opted by the problems, fears, and follies of the adults around them. Like Jordie in *Giant,* children have had the tokens of their celebrations snatched from them and have been forced to participate in the world of their parents' insecurities.

Hollywood's rituals project and reflect so much about the culture of which Hollywood is a part that we begin to see the America of children, according to the movies, as increasingly dangerous, sad, and disappointing. The difference between Francie Nolan's bittersweet graduation and that of the world-weary friends in *Reality Bites* is the difference between hope and despair, between trust and suspicion, between meaningful rituals and empty ritual occasions.

From infant baptism through college graduations, children's ceremonial rites have been portrayed most often as difficult or heartbreaking points on film which correspond more to the difficulties and heartbreaks of adults than to the children themselves. Children, whether infants or teenagers, are most often victims of larger conflicts in American movies made since 1945. As Hollywood uses the ceremonial rites of its child characters to suggest and evaluate the worlds of its adult characters, the films have become less sentimental toward children and more inclined to show an America where children's lives and their ritual occasions often suggest the opposite of what they are meant to celebrate. On screen, birthdays mean loneliness or poverty; graduations mean aimlessness and cynicism; sacred rites have nothing to do with children's souls.

Near the conclusion of the 1990 production of *Last Exit to Brooklyn,* a small, powerful American production which is set during a dock workers' strike in 1952 Brooklyn, we watch a small baby boy being baptized in a Roman Catholic church. The camera hugs this sweet baby for a moment, then moves on to show us his godparents, who are holding him, and his proud grandparents standing by. Finally, we see that his parents are also present, standing all smiles in front of the altar wearing their wedding finery. This is their wedding day.

This combined ritual occasion is one of the most peaceful, genuinely touching moments in a relatively grim film. It also represents a rare but significant moment in a Hollywood film, where a celebration of a baby's baptism is truly the point where the life of a child overshadows, if only for a moment, the world of the adults around him, for the camera and the narrative of the film privilege the baby's ritual, not that of his parents.

The wedding ceremony that we don't see in *Last Exit to Brooklyn,* however, is a wedding of two teenagers themselves, who have married because of their son's birth. Like so many American films made since 1945, this film forces us to question the values and importance of the very institutions it portrays: religion, law, education, and marriage become shifting signifiers in the movies during the second half of the twentieth century. The wedding in *Last Exit to Brooklyn* is one of thousands of wedding scenes that will allow us to watch the children of Hollywood films marry. Whether their weddings mean more than their earlier ritual occasions remains to be seen.

3

WEDDING CELEBRATIONS

Stanley T. Banks (Spencer Tracy) is slumped in his armchair in the middle of his living room, which is cluttered with the debris of what seems to have been a lavish party. He massages his aching feet, lifts his head wearily, and addresses his audience: "I would like to say a few words about weddings." He will say more than a few words, of course, before he has finished telling us how it feels to be the father of the bride. For his audience, Stanley's story about his daughter's wedding serves as a means to an end. The tale of his life as an American father includes a rite as traditional to American film as his daughter's ceremony is to American culture: the wedding celebration.

As he takes us through his version of his daughter's courtship and engagement, and as we experience Kay Banks's (Elizabeth Taylor's) elaborate wedding celebration in *Father of the Bride,* we begin to realize that what Stanley is really telling us is not the simple story of how his daughter became married, but of how he had to adapt to changes in his life which he did not fully understand. We become aware early in the movie that this is really *his* story. He confides to us:

Someday in the far future, I may be able to remember [my daughter's wedding] with tender indulgence, but not now. I always used to think that marriage was a simple affair—boy and girl meet, they fall in love, get married, they have babies, eventually the babies grow up and meet other babies and fall in love and get married, and on and on and on. Looked at that way, it's not only simple, it's downright monotonous. But I was wrong. I figured without the wedding.

Through his often exasperated voice-overs and his grimaces, we sense Stanley's reluctance to understand or accept his daughter's choices. Although he tells his story in a whimsical, humorous way, we understand that he is trying to define the world he lives in, a world where he is trying to survive life—and parenthood—in a post-World War II suburban environment where much of what he experiences rings false to him, and where he is sure of nothing.

Father of the Bride was certainly not the first American movie to include a wedding celebration scene.[1] American audiences have been the honored guests at innumerable weddings in Hollywood movies since early silent films. From epic dramas like *Out of Africa* (1985) to comedies like *Lovers and Other Strangers* (1970), from musicals like *Oklahoma!* (1955) to horror movies like *The Bride of Frankenstein* (1935), Hollywood has provided us with a variety of marriage celebrations. We have watched elopements (*New York, New York,* 1977), lavish fairy-tale affairs (*The Sound of Music,* 1965), and interrupted ceremonies (*Private Benjamin,* 1980). We have seen couples marry in the midst of war (*Sayonara,* 1957), in Western cowtowns (*High Noon,* 1952), in ancient cathedrals (*Royal Wedding,* 1951), in the woods (*Days of Heaven,* 1978), and moments before the death penalty is to be carried out on the couple (*The African Queen,* 1951). As audiences, we have experienced these weddings as opening scenes (*The Young Philadelphians,* 1959), as flashbacks (*Fried Green Tomatoes,* 1991), and as concluding scenes (*The Best Years of Our Lives,* 1946).

A wedding celebration—on film or otherwise—combines highly conventionalized ceremony with the idiosyncrasies of its major participants. Because of the inherent tension between the universal and the serendipitous, weddings are well suited to the complicated nature of storytelling through film. Depending on the directors' motives and decisions, audiences experience a variety of powerful responses to the weddings we see on film. We can be standing at the altar with the wedding party, or among the other invited guests, or as detached outsiders when we see weddings on film. Where we are in relation to the marrying couple helps us to understand much of what we see in a film.

As anthropologists have pointed out, public celebrations often suggest a paradox for all people involved, either as onlookers or participants: amidst the pomp of public display and resolution of some kind, there are also signs of conflicting elements, often opposites. Certainly a wedding, with its opposing male/female, public/private, ritualistic/individualized elements, represents a most significant and complicated ceremonial rite which filmmakers have long used for its power on screen. When we watch a wedding on film, we feel many things at the same time: we rejoice, or we cringe with embarrassment, or we feel a sense of doom. We begin to understand both universal truths and unique characteristics of whatever culture's ritual is being presented to us. We begin to distinguish tradition from fad, and institution from intuition. We recognize weddings as formalities and as genuine rituals.

Wedding celebrations serve as significant gauges to how we will interpret and judge characters and circumstances—indeed, entire worlds—in the movies. Through weddings, we can identify any number of powerful signs and signals about the worlds in the movies. Director Vincent Minnelli's *Father of the Bride,* as light-hearted as it might have seemed when it was released in 1950, presents one of the clearest examples of a Hollywood production that uses a wedding celebration to help the audience identify and assimilate characteristics of a segment of American culture.

In his study of American films of the 1950s, Douglas Brode discusses how the traditional wedding we see in this film is used to expose to the audience a set of conflicting images: ". . . while [*Father of the Bride*] lovingly portrayed the people and their foibles, it mixed that tenderness with a satiric point of view on middle-class customs that, at moments, was almost savage" (28).

Finally optimistic in its point of view, *Father of the Bride* seems to suggest that the sacrament of marriage is strong enough to endure the conflicts and costs (monetary, physical, and emotional) imposed by public and personal expectations of the event. Yet again, love conquers all, and the most formal of human rituals of love survives.

Father of the Bride "set the pace for many films that followed" because it was "the first American film to be set, quite clearly, in suburbia" (28). Since the 1950s, and especially since the 1960s, the rise of American suburban culture has become an easy and popular target among Hollywood filmmakers, and weddings have served as an effective kind of "ammunition" most often used to attack the hypocrisies of that segment of American society. Where *Father of the Bride* suggests that the accoutrements and lavish preparations needed for an affluent suburban wedding threaten the core ritual, the institution remains inviolate. There may be no better way to understand the power of the wedding celebration in American film than to look at how films since *Father of the Bride* use weddings to highlight what Hollywood sees as the superficial vulgarity of the middle and upper-middle classes in American society.

One of the most memorable wedding scenes from an American film is a wedding that we never really celebrate, that of Elaine Robinson (Katharine Ross). When Benjamin Braddock (Dustin Hoffman) intrudes on Elaine's traditional wedding near the end of *The Graduate,* we see this fiasco from several different perspectives. We watch with Elaine while Benjamin, standing crucifix-like, screams for her from the balcony of the church. We stand with Benjamin above and watch the wedding party and Elaine's parents mouthing threats and curses at Benjamin. We see Elaine run out of the church while Benjamin jams the door behind her with a cross, and our parting shot is of Benjamin, in his street clothes, and Elaine, in her torn bridal gown, sitting tentatively at the back of a public bus, moving away from the church and from us.

In the spirit of *It Happened One Night* (1934) and *The Philadelphia Story* (1940), *The Graduate* concludes with a bride defying the tradition of her own wedding ceremony by deserting her groom. Also like the brides in these comedies of the 1930s, Elaine Robinson leaves behind a comfortable, predictable, upper-class life. What distinguishes the interrupted wedding in

The Graduate, however, is that we are not convinced of the reasons for Elaine's decision to run away with Benjamin. We recognize self-knowledge and true romance in Claudette Colbert's and Katharine Hepburn's characters; in both films, the families of the brides fully endorse the rebellion. The renounced wedding, we know, will lead to a proper wedding where a meaningful ritual of love and bonding will be enacted. We recognize ambiguity, confusion, and anger in Elaine Robinson. Does she love Benjamin? We're not sure, but we know that she hates her mother, Mrs. Robinson (Anne Bancroft). We understand the intensity with which she loathes her mother, and her mother's way of life, most pointedly by her choice to disrupt her own wedding.[2]

Several other Hollywood films of the 1960s use wedding celebration scenes to help us identify conflict between generations or clashes among several sets of social values in American culture. As in *The Graduate,* other wedding scenes help us to sympathize with characters who are only on the periphery of the weddings, or who really do not fit into the socioeconomic classes presented to us. We watch these celebrations through the eyes of these outsiders, and we see what they see. Segments of American culture are defined for us as contradictory, hypocritical, and vulgar.

Goodbye Columbus (1970) and *The Heartbreak Kid* (1972), movies which came out shortly after *The Graduate,* include blatantly vulgar wedding scenes, and both of these films expand the wedding scenes to include lengthy reception scenes. In a sense, they allow us to see the wedding reception which Elaine Robinson did not have, and in doing so, suggest that the wedding being celebrated was no more than an empty formal occasion rather than a transformative or redemptive experience.

In *Goodbye Columbus,* Neil Klugman (Richard Benjamin) has chosen to spend his summer vacation away from his library clerking position, with the suburban family of his girlfriend, Radcliffe coed Brenda Patimkin (Ali McGraw). Neil's bookish ways and urban mentality have caused trouble between Brenda and her parents, yet he has reluctantly agreed to attend the wedding of Brenda's brother Ron and his fiancee Harriette. By the time of the wedding scene, we have been prepared for a supreme clash of values. We know that Neil is a mature, independent man who has served in the military and is worldly in ways that Brenda is not. We also know, from scenes which show him clerking in the public library, that he does not share many of the values of Brenda's nouveau riche family. When we attend Ron Patimkin's wedding with Neil, we understand that he is skeptical of many of the standards and institutions which the Patimkins hold dear. When we attend the reception, we see more vividly the aspects of the Patimkins' way of life which appall Neil.

Our first image of the reception is a shot of a liver pate duck being beheaded. With one violent gesture, the father of the groom shoves the entire pate head into his mouth. From this point on, we are subjected to any number of shots of celebrating guests imbibing, eating, and dancing at various stages of excess. The women are dressed in sequins and glitter and clash before ours and Neil's eyes; the men are talking about business profits and the value of real estate.

We are uncomfortable at this reception, for reasons that have very little to do with the wedding. In fact, the bride and groom are not particularly important to us, except to further our response that this is a group of people who, compared to Neil, seem limited and shallow. Ron Patimkin, ex-basketball star at Ohio State, has proved himself to be a mental midget. His bride, on finding out that Neil is a library clerk, responds vacuously that "it must be nice to get first-crack at all of the best-sellers." We are allied with Neil, isolated with him in horror at the vulgarity and superficiality of the world of the Patimkins. When Neil's and Brenda's relationship dissolves in the next (and final) scene of the film, we are not surprised, nor particularly disappointed. The wedding reception has served to assure us that neither Neil nor we want to be part of the world of Brenda Patimkin. This wedding has helped us to understand that in Hollywood films, bad weddings can be indications of further bad relationships, and often more bad weddings, as *The Heartbreak Kid* demonstrates.

In *The Heartbreak Kid,* a film which has much in common with both *The Graduate* and *Goodbye Columbus,* we meet Leonard (Charles Grodin) just before he marries Lila (Jeannie Berlin). Theirs is a small, traditional Jewish wedding in New York, where we immediately notice that things are not quite right: the musicians are amateurs who can barely keep in tune, the room is too warm, and everyone seems uncomfortable. We have a basic sense that the wedding is not quite right here. The suggestion of disharmony in this ceremony is immediately reinforced in the next sequence in the film, when Leonard and Lila take off in their car for a honeymoon in Miami Beach. Instead of a romantic idyll, their honeymoon becomes a disappointing farce when Lila spends too much time sunbathing, and takes to her bed with second-degree burns. The suspicions we may have had because of this couple's uncomfortable wedding have been confirmed for us. Leonard's and Lila's honeymoon is over, and their marriage looks to be in peril as well.

An irritated and irritable Leonard goes out on the beach alone, where he meets Kelly (Cybill Shepard), a wealthy young coed on vacation with her parents. As his new wife's sunburn heals slowly in their hotel room, Leonard begins courting Kelly, who is unaware that Leonard is on his honeymoon. Unbeknownst to Kelly or her family, Leonard deserts Lila (we never see her again in the film), and he follows Kelly and her family back to her hometown in Minnesota.

From this point on, Leonard's quest is to woo and win the beautiful Kelly, despite (or perhaps because of) the differences in their backgrounds. After painful attempts to be accepted by Kelly and her possessive father (Eddie Albert), Leonard does marry Kelly. We are in attendance at his second wedding, just as we were when he married Lila.

As soon as we see the elegant Kelly on the arm of her silver-haired father, walking down the aisle of what looks to be a large Protestant church, we are reminded of Lila. In one the first scenes of the movie, she walked clumsily between her parents, the three of them negotiating their way toward Leonard among narrow rows of folding chairs. When we hear the band at Kelly and Leonard's reception playing "Close to You," we are reminded that a smaller, less skilled dance band played this same song at Lila and Leonard's wedding. We remember that the guests at the first wedding danced and sang "Hava Nagila"; at the second wedding, the guests want to know about Leonard's profession (he has none), and they discuss business deals and finances.

The Heartbreak Kid combines the young-man-who-will-stop-at-nothing aspect of *The Graduate* with the young-man-from-the-wrong-side-of-town story from *Goodbye Columbus.* What distinguishes *The Heartbreak Kid* from these other movies is that unlike Benjamin or Neil, who are not members of the weddings, Leonard, the character to whom the audience is most closely allied, marries not once, but twice. By watching two wedding celebration scenes, we begin to see the contrasts between the world Leonard has forsaken and the world into which he has entered. The final scene of this film shows Leonard sitting on a sofa during his wedding reception, discussing his aspirations with two bored adolescent wedding guests. We have heard him discussing this same topic at least twice before at this wedding, and, as his previous adult listeners did, his young listeners get up and leave him sitting alone at his own wedding.

We don't blame them. Leonard is truly the odd man out. He has participated in two weddings as the groom, but he has never truly married. In some ways, he seems a character waiting for the transformative power of the ritual to change him; what he does not ever grasp is that ritual occasions do not transform, and true rituals gain their power by linking real changes in the human spirit of the individual and group to a transcendent spirit or ideal.[3]

The Heartbreak Kid is certainly not the only Hollywood production to use two weddings to help us distinguish aspects of the worlds of film. Several movies open and close with wedding scenes, including *It Happened One Night, The Palm Beach Story* (1942), *Private Benjamin* (1980), and *Mystic Pizza* (1988). As in *The Heartbreak Kid,* this symmetrical bracketing of celebrations lets us compare characters and situations in ways we could not do without the combination of ceremony and circumstance that two weddings allow.

A pair of weddings in one film can serve several functions. In *It Happened One Night,* we learn to recognize true love by seeing the bride leave her own wedding a second time—this time for Clark Gable. In *The Palm Beach Story,* a mystery is cleared up for us by watching a wedding ceremony for the second time. In two Hollywood productions of the 1980s, *Private Benjamin* and *Mystic Pizza,* we become aware of growth and self-knowledge, especially in the brides, by watching opening and closing scenes of weddings.

Judy Benjamin's first wedding is an elegant, joyous affair. She seems happy enough; her biggest concern at her reception is that the upholsterer she hired has covered her new husband's ottoman with the wrong fabric. We quickly realize, however, that Judy's world is not as bright as it first appears. During her reception, her attorney husband (Albert Brooks) leaves her to take care of some business on the phone, and her father expresses more interest in a televised sports event than he does in Judy. When her groom dies suddenly of a heart attack on their wedding night, and she is faced with major decisions about her future, Judy begins to understand what we have understood since her wedding celebration scene. Her life has been defined for her by men, to whom she is truly nothing more that a princess. Her elaborate wedding was a formal ritual occasion, but she has no marriage to accompany it. Lost in her own grief and pity, alone in a motel room, Judy succumbs to the lure of television advertising, and joins the army.

We experience life in the army with Private Benjamin, where she survives basic training by her own wits, thus gaining a degree of self-worth she has never known before. We travel with her on her first assignment to France, where she meets and falls in love with a wealthy young Frenchman (Armand Assante). She consents to marry him, and we are all ready for the second-chance happy ending we know that Judy deserved at the beginning of the film. However, for reasons that seem all too familiar to her (and to us), Judy leaves the scene of her own wedding. She has been through a wedding before, and has since become mature enough to recognize that a wedding is a formal ritual occasion that does not necessarily mean happiness. When Judy runs off into the beautiful French landscape, we celebrate her disrupted wedding with her. When she throws off her wedding veil and rejects her wedding day, we see how much she has grown. The contrast of the two Judy Benjamins is clear to us because we have watched her two weddings, and we know that she has learned a lesson because of these ritual occasions: weddings are static formal occasions, not transformative or transcendent moments. Judy Benjamin has come of age.

In *Mystic Pizza,* we have a similar response to the second wedding of Jojo (Lili Taylor). Her first wedding ceremony is interrupted because, out of desperation and nervousness, she faints at the altar. She later confesses to her two friends Daisy (Julia Roberts) and Kat (Annabeth Gish) that she panicked during the wedding. She is not ready to become the wife of her fisherman boyfriend until he understands that she wants to maintain her own identity and some sense of freedom.

Jojo's is only one of three stories of the coming-of-age process in *Mystic Pizza.* Yet, just as we are exposed to Jojo's conflict as the first scene of the film, so we see her problem resolved in the final sequence: her second—and successful—wedding celebration. When Jojo finally marries Billy, we feel joy for her and for her friends, both of whom have also resolved their own problems by maturing during the course of the film. It is during this final joyous celebration of Jojo's wedding that we celebrate love and community, growth and promise.

The final wedding scene in *Mystic Pizza* illustrates another way in which wedding celebrations become important to audiences: these scenes make the audience aware of the cultural boundaries of movies. Jojo, Daisy and Kat are all local girls who work at a pizza parlor in the resort town of Mystic, Connecticut, and throughout the film, there is a subplot which involves the conflict between the local Portuguese-American working-class culture of these young women, and the upper-class clientele—

those wealthy WASPS who summer on the coast. The audience resolves this conflict at the same time that we resolve the others in the movie—in the final wedding celebration scene. We watch all three women and their friends and families participate in dances and sing songs which may seem foreign to us, unless we know about Portuguese-American culture. Whether we understand their culture or not, we do recognize that Jojo, Daisy and Kat are part of a rich cultural heritage which is made clear to us by this joyous wedding celebration.

Other American films also include two wedding scenes which help us to gauge growth or change in characters, and which also serve to portray and define character, community, and ethnicity for an audience. Certainly the most powerful example of an American movie that includes two ethnic weddings is *The Godfather,* which offers two weddings so different that we understand much about the film and the world of the Sicilian-American Corleones because of them.

At the opening of *The Godfather,* Connie Corleone has just been married, and her family is hosting a lavish reception on the compound grounds. We meet all of the Corleones at this celebration, and our first impressions of them are significant. The entire reception sequence (one of the longest of any Hollywood film—twenty-five minutes) is a series of cuts from inside the house (where Don Corleone is taking care of business in his office) to the festivities outside. We are forced to adjust our eyesight to watch this sequence because the contrast between what goes on inside and what goes on outside is visually stunning. The Don's office is dark, with Venetian blinds barely cracked, and every time we move back to the reception, we are in the bright sunlight of the Corleone estate.

We must, of course, adjust more than our eyesight as we try to understand the world of the Corleones. As in the case of the other ritual scenes studied in this work, this series of wedding reception scenes serves as our best guide to an understanding of conflict within the family and identification of characteristics of the Corleone family members. The Don spends most of his time granting favors to his Sicilian-American friends; among these favors on his daughter's wedding day is the promise to make a group of young thugs "suffer." Sonny Corleone spends part of the day with one of his sister's bridesmaids, enjoying a quick sexual encounter in an upstairs bedroom of the Corleone home while his wife sits outside at the reception. And Michael, the young returned war hero in military uniform, spends his afternoon trying not to represent himself as a member of the Corleone family. He tells his girlfriend Kay, "That's my family, Kay, not me."

It is during this first sequence of a ritual occasion that we begin to judge the strengths and weaknesses of the family we will come to know so well. Vito Corleone is proud, commanding, and at the same time, a family man who glides gracefully across the dance floor with his daughter. Sonny is guided by passion, and he makes rash decisions. His timing is never quite right, as we note when Tom Hagen has to knock on a bedroom door to summon Sonny to his father's office during Sonny's sexual liaison. And Michael seems genuinely different from the other Corleones in this first scene. We not only learn that he is a veteran, but that he is college-educated and worldly in a way that none of his relatives are. We also recognize, even before he makes his first appearance, that he is his father's favorite son.

These are significant characteristics of the Corleone men which we can identify only because of this wedding celebration of a female Corleone. It is not insignificant that the Corleone women remain outside the house, away from the men's world, throughout the scene. The Corleone women are always outsiders in this film—indeed, throughout the entire *Godfather* epic. Vito's nameless wife dances with her husband, sings a Sicilian song with the band, but never says one line in this wedding sequence. We see Connie only from distances, always dancing or laughing or posing for wedding pictures. Of the Corleone women, only Kay, the ethnic "outsider" whom Michael insists on including in the Corleone family photo, speaks more than a few lines, and she mostly asks questions.

Just as we begin to understand the personalities of the Corleone men during this wedding sequence, we also come to realize the absence of strong female presences in the Corleone world. Women are mothers, wives, daughters, or sexual objects who are silent shadows or who behave in ways which complement their men. Through the opening wedding scene, we realize that these celebrating women help us to establish a paradigm for *The Godfather,* and for the *Godfather* trilogy: the Corleone men celebrate their religious traditions and cultural heritage while they defy or distort them; they espouse family values while they destroy families; they both value and abuse their women, just as they value and abuse other institutions in the world around them.[4]

As noted in the discussion of rituals in *The Godfather* epic, Michael's simple, graceful wedding to Apollonia later in the film underscores the elaborate complexities of Connie's wedding for us. Michael's wedding is shown in straightforward narrative— no cuts back and forth between an indoor setting and an outdoor setting—and we have a significant context in which to place his love story with Apollonia, because we have watched their courtship. The two weddings indeed serve to help us understand the contrast between New World Corleones and Old World Corleones. What we understand is that Michael, uncomfortable at his sister's New World wedding, is his most natural and happiest in the Old World. In *The Godfather,* Michael becomes the only child of Vito Corleone who can possibly bridge the gaps— between New World and Old, between his family and the Family. We understand Michael's position because we watch his behavior at these two weddings.

The two weddings have their dark sides, of course. The Corleones celebrate Connie's wedding on the lawn of her father's grand estate, but also within a walled compound, surrounded by an elaborate series of dark cars and bodyguards with guns. Violence in this wedding sequence is never far from the surface, nor far from the wedding celebration itself; at one point, Sonny Corleone roughs up a photographer and destroys his camera just a few feet away from the wedding celebration. Michael's Sicilian wedding, for all its innocence and apparent transformative power, is also guarded by gunmen, one of whom will kill Apollonia in a failed attempt on Michael's life.

These weddings are complex occasions where the promise of marriage and the ritual of love are shadowed by the lives of the participants. Where the wedding in *Father of the Bride* nearly collapses under the weight of the formalities, in *The Godfather* the formalities are integral parts of the ritual of marriage; it is the flawed human participants who darken and threaten the rite.

The weddings in *The Godfather* are matched in epic proportions by one other American film in which a wedding becomes our entrance into a world of ethnicity, loyalty, and betrayal. Like *The Godfather*, *The Deer Hunter* shows a wedding where marriage is not the focus of the ritual occasion being presented, but other relationships are developed during the wedding celebration. *The Deer Hunter* begins with a lengthy series of scenes (more than an hour) which include a Ukrainian wedding ceremony and reception. By the time this long wedding celebration ends, we have been prepared for much of what will come in the film. Early in the wedding preparation scene, we learn that groom Steven (John Savage) and his two best friends Mike (Robert DeNiro) and Nick (Christopher Walken) are to leave for Vietnam the following day. By the time the wedding celebration ends, and Nick says to Mike, "if anything happens over there, don't leave me, man," we have been assured, by attending this long wedding party, that something will happen.

As in *The Godfather*, the audience is often the only guest to notice certain details or behaviors at the wedding in *The Deer Hunter*. We are privy to any number of secrets that will become increasingly important to us as the story moves away from its Pennsylvania setting and to Vietnam. At the wedding, for instance, we alone notice that although Nick and Mike seem very close, there seems to be a tension between them concerning Nick's fiancee Linda (Meryl Streep). Both men are attracted to her, and during the reception, the significant looks which pass between Linda and Mike are made very clear to the audience. Also, only we notice the drops of red wine which fall on the bride's white bodice during the couple's ritual drink from the double wine vessel. This close-up of her stained bodice is for our benefit, of course, and we sense doom for the happy couple immediately.[5]

We see the women who belong to the men of *The Deer Hunter* most often in the wedding sequence, just as we see the Corleone women most during the ritual scenes. We recognize that in *The Deer Hunter,* the women also have all the marks of victims, and that it is through the women that we understand much of the dynamic between or among the men. Certainly Linda (at first Nick's fiancee, and later Mike's tentative lover) stands out during the wedding scene as a significant character, not just because we see that both men are attracted to her, but because she represents a sort of bridge to us—a connection between the two soldiers and their hometown, a fusion of Old World and New World ways of life. Significantly, while the wedding party is preparing for the wedding, Linda is beaten by her drunken immigrant father while she is wearing her bridesmaid's gown. She packs a bag and moves into her boyfriend's home. To us, she has chosen a solution to her problem that reflects America in the 1960s, not the Ukrainian values of her family. Also, while she celebrates at the wedding, we can't help but notice that she is more comfortable sitting at the bar drinking a beer than she is carrying the bride's wedding crown. Because of attention paid to her during this wedding sequence, Linda becomes a paradoxical character who embodies some of the most crucial conflicts and uncertainties in the film. She helps introduce us to questions of loyalty, tradition, violence, and longing during this wedding.[6]

Beyond Linda, there are many more details in the opening sequence of *The Deer Hunter* that will haunt us later. The three friends Mike, Nick, and Steven try to carry on a brazen conversation with a uniformed Green Beret who will not look at them. At those later points in the film when all three of these now-soldiers are isolated—Steven in the hospital, Mike in a motel room, and Nick in the gambling dens of Saigon—we will remember this lone Green Beret at the wedding.

As the film moves into the Vietnam sequences, and the three friends are first held prisoner and then separated in their attempts to escape, we might remember that Steven has always seemed more vulnerable than Mike and Nick and that he has always depended on their strength. After we see the paraplegic Steven in the hospital, we may remember that he clumsily fell to the floor during a Ukrainian dance at his wedding, or we may remember Nick's parting advice to him as he left for his honeymoon—"hang tough"—when we watch Steven being lifted from a Vietnam battlefield into a helicopter.

The wedding sequence in *The Deer Hunter* then, helps to educate us about the world that Steven, Mike, and Nick are leaving. After we have moved through this wedding with them, we understand what is important to them, and because of this scene, we also understand aspects of their lives that they do not understand themselves. Mike displays a tendency to isolate himself, even during the wedding reception; Nick takes many small risks, constantly pushing himself, and Steven seems unlucky and fragile.

We are not particularly celebratory at the conclusion of the wedding in *The Deer Hunter,* which attests to the power of this scene as a ritual occasion. We have gotten to know the characters and their families, and they all seem unhappy, naive, doomed. After the party has ended, Mike laments to Nick as the two of them sit alone in the dark, "Everything's going so fast." Nick does not seem to understand this comment, but we do. We have spent a long, festive day with these men, and we now anticipate that "things" will go even faster for them.[7]

Although the wedding scenes in *The Godfather* and *The Deer Hunter* may represent two of the most powerful projections of weddings in American film, they share a significant characteristic with many other wedding scenes in other movies. What we come to understand about almost all wedding scenes in Hollywood productions is that, like scenes of other ritual occasions in American film, scenes of weddings rarely tell us how happy a marrying couple is, or how good the uniting families feel. Weddings scenes often are not at all about the marrying couple, who are usually incidental to the films. Their weddings do not represent transformative events, but are instead important matrixes for other developments in the movies.

There are countless American films that use weddings to further plot or identify conflict within or among characters.[8] In *Giant,* Jordan Benedict (Rock Hudson) travels from Texas to Maryland to try to reunite with his estranged wife Leslie (Elizabeth Taylor). He arrives at the front door of Leslie's father's home precisely as Leslie's sister is being married in the living room, and he moves slowly and silently to a point where he can see Leslie, who is participating as the matron of honor. Leslie senses that Jordan is standing behind her, and, as the wedding service comes to a close, she turns around slowly to face him. As the wedding march plays, the two of them embrace in a passionate kiss of reconciliation. In *Working Girl* (1988), Tess (Melanie Griffith) attends a wedding celebration to which she has not been invited in order to make a business deal, and she successfully demonstrates her business acumen by describing a merger to the bride's father while they dance together at the reception. In *The Accidental Tourist* (1988), Macon Leary (William Hurt) and his ex-wife Sarah (Kathleen Turner) serve as witnesses for his sister's wedding ceremony. As they stand beside the bride and groom, listening carefully to the minister, they begin looking at each other. Shortly after this scene, they rekindle their relationship.

Often, wedding scenes in American movies allow us to see the opposite of what we expect to see on screen. In fact, many wedding scenes, especially those which introduce a film, show us conflict, unhappiness, or doom. In *The Group,* Kay (Joanna Pettet) and Harald (Larry Hagman) marry early in the film, with Kay's group of Vassar "sisters" in attendance. During the wedding breakfast, as the Group sits around the table chatting and celebrating, we learn enough about the personalities of these women to begin to anticipate complications in their stories. There is a giggler, a serious medical student, a socialite, and a Democrat among them, and they argue, drink, and compete for the attentions of the eligible young men at this party. Also during this wedding scene, Harald makes one too many jokes at Kay's expense, and we, like her embarrassed friends, may suspect that Harald will not be an ideal mate.

60 · *Reel Rituals*

Wedding scenes can also suggest anxiety. *The Best Years of Our Lives* (1946) ends with a very agitated Fred Perry (Dana Andrews), consenting with an almost-clenched fist to marry Peggy Stevenson (Teresa Wright), at the wedding of his war buddy Homer (Harold Russell). We experience fear, perhaps bordering on horror, while we watch the lovely Jewish wedding of two characters in 1933 Berlin in *Cabaret* (1972). In *Days of Heaven* (1978), we know that the marriage of the lonely wheat rancher (Sam Shepard) and the drifter (Brooke Adams) is ill-fated, because we know that she has married the wealthy rancher not out of love for him, but as part of an elaborate scam concocted with her lover (Richard Gere) to inherit his property. And the film *Unforgiven* (1992) opens with a sequence in which a Mexican wedding is interrupted by gunfire and becomes a blood bath.[9]

The example from *Unforgiven* suggests another convention of Hollywood weddings. Since the 1950s, really since *Father of the Bride,* American movies have most often depicted weddings that represent a white, Judeo-Christian tradition, almost always from the middle to upper economic classes. Although we see married couples from other ethnic or racial groups represented on film, rarely, until the 1980s, do we watch them marry. This should come as no surprise; mainstream Hollywood productions most often represent dominant cultures, both in terms of film production and in the films themselves. As the complexion of Hollywood has slowly begun to change, especially since the 1980s, the storytelling nature of film has changed as well—albeit slowly.

Of all of the rituals portrayed in the movies, perhaps wedding celebrations have reflected the demographic changes in Hollywood most obviously. *Unforgiven* uses an ethnic wedding in a traditional Hollywood manner: to show minority populations as victims of someone else's battles. Minority characters have generally served three purposes: stereotyping, passive victimization, or comic relief. Because we have seen that weddings in American film are most often used to tell us something about the hypocrisies of the white culture, ethnic or racial weddings have little relevance to most mainstream Hollywood productions, and almost never appear.[10]

The Color Purple (1985) was one of the first major Hollywood productions to feature a wedding between blacks, although there are a few earlier film depictions. There are recent American productions that allow us to experience other types of weddings where the celebrants are also important characters who are not portrayed as marginal victims or devices: *The Mambo Kings* (1992), *Mi Familia* (1995), *Come See the Paradise* (1990), and *Heaven and Earth* (1991).

In the last two of these movies, we see interracial couples marry, which also is rare but has its own history in Hollywood cinema: the films *Sayonara* (1957) and *Bridge to the Sun* (1961) both include interracial wedding scenes. In *Sayonara,* a film that takes place in Japan during the Korean War, Army private Joe Kelly (Red Buttons) marries his Japanese fiancee Katsumi (Miyoshi Umeki) against orders; the U.S. Army, we learn, strongly discourages American G.I.s from marrying Japanese women. Kelly's commanding officer Major Lloyd Gruver (Marlon Brando) reluctantly consents to be the couple's witness, and we watch their short ceremony, conducted tersely by an Army chaplain in his private office. After the ceremony, Major Gruver, surprised by the chaplain's harsh tones and abrupt manner, asks "Do you always conduct wedding ceremonies this way?" "We try to discourage weddings among the troops," the chaplain answers curtly. The wedding has been overshadowed by the political realities and prejudices of a world which will make life difficult for this newlywed couple—so hard, in fact, that they will commit double suicide near the end of the film. Their wedding is our first clue to the cruelties and hypocrisies awaiting them.[11]

When we attend weddings in Hollywood films, no matter who is marrying, or when, or where, we can count on the kinds of clues we see in *Sayonara* to help us anticipate later developments. We can expect that a wedding means something quite opposite of what the ritual implies, and that what we need to know from a wedding scene is not about the marriage—Connie

Corleone, after all, is not who we remember when we think of her wedding. A wedding on film most often signals a complication, not a simplification, a problem, not a solution.

Of all of the ritual occasions represented in this study, none has a more complex or compelling history than wedding celebrations. They are Hollywood's most popular, versatile and abused film ritual, reduced to mere formalities that are more profane than sacred, more generative of conflict than resolution. Weddings represent one of the most sacred rites in any culture, yet in Hollywood films they become generic signals for something other than the sacred. Weddings are rarely reasons for us to celebrate in a film; they often give us reasons to worry.

Although—or perhaps because—weddings can be used and abused so readily in the movies, they are rarely the subjects themselves of American films (even Stanley Banks' story in *Father of the Bride* is about himself, not about his daughter's marriage). Robert Altman's *A Wedding* (1978) is one of the only American films in which the wedding celebration represents the entire plot of the film. In its uneven expansion of this ritual occasion from plot device to full-length treatment, *A Wedding* demonstrates just how powerful and valuable the ritual occasion of the wedding really is—not in *A Wedding* itself, but when imbedded in other films.

The aspects of American culture that other wedding scenes bring to our attention—especially vulgarity and hypocrisy—make us painfully uncomfortable in *A Wedding,* which presents us with a pointed caricature of a wedding day. The officiating priest is senile. The bride (whose name is "Muffin" and whose parents are "Snooks" and "Tulip") has braces on her teeth. Her groom has impregnated her sister/maid of honor, "Buffy." During the reception, the groom's grandmother dies, and his mother, an elegant, erratic heroin addict married to a lecherous doctor, leaves the reception to be "medicated."

Like several other Altman films (*Nashville* in 1975; *Quintet* in 1979; *Ready to Wear* in 1994), *A Wedding* is complicated and yet plotless; it is an accumulation of conversations and vignettes which the audience must struggle to distinguish. When we watch this movie, we are attending a two-hour wedding celebration from beginning to end. Unfortunately, although we are with this wedding party for two hours, we never really know much about any of the participants, and we are among families and guests we may not particularly like. At its worst, *A Wedding* becomes a tedious, cruel parody of a ritual occasion that unravels before our eyes, deconstructing itself into a series of sight gags and meaningless symbols of the wedding rite.[12] However, by contrasting the failure of the ritual occasion in *A Wedding,* we become more sensitive to the power and versatility of the wedding celebration in other movies.

A Wedding reminds us that we do not need to watch a simulated wedding celebration in its entirety in order to understand the value of weddings to American film; when wedding rituals are portrayed anywhere in the movies, they are significant and powerful gauges to our understanding. Indeed, Stanley Banks was wise to warn us not to "figure without the wedding" when he spoke to us in *Father of the Bride.* Weddings usually help us understand much of what we are experiencing in a film, and, like other ritual occasions, are so familiar to us that they are easy to take for granted. We must watch carefully, however, because weddings usually signal dissonance, not resolution. For instance, in *Ragtime* (1981), Coalhouse Walker, Jr. (Howard Rollins) and his fiancee Sarah (Debbie Allen) have planned their wedding, and her beautiful white dress is ready. But before their wedding day, Sarah is beaten to death by a white mob. Instead of a wedding, we see an elaborate and beautiful funeral in a Harlem church, with Sarah lying in her coffin in her wedding dress, and Coalhouse Walker motivated, out of anger and grief, to plan his own violent revenge against those he blames for Sarah's death.

For a moment, these ritual occasions seem interchangable to the audience, as indeed they are meant to; we become aware in this scene that a wedding and a funeral are both ritual occasions where the line between the sacred and the profane becomes blurred. In American films, the difference between a wedding and funeral can be a very small one, as *Ragtime* demonstrates. And, like so much of what we see on screen,

Hollywood films demand that we adjust our expectations because weddings and funerals both might betray our expectations of rituals. As we have seen, Hollywood weddings can upset us by implying failure or sorrow, and transcendence and luminosity rarely appear. Funerals, our most fundamental and emotion-laden ritual occasions, both literally and figuratively ground us in the mundane.

4

WAKES, FUNERALS, AND BURIALS

In her study of rites of passage, anthropologist Barbara Myerhoff asks the very cogent question, "Does a rite of passage always cause its participants to think about their condition?" (117). She answers:

> Some anthropologists argue that rituals make individuals less likely to do so. By keeping them busy in the obsessive, formal, repetitive activity that rituals require, consciousness and questioning may be inhibited rather than encouraged. (117-18)

Myerhoff refines this answer further by using an example of a funeral. A person swept up in the planning of the details of a funeral may not have time to think about mortality, yet "on another deeper, less verbal, less cognitive level, we understand something about our own death in contemplating and enacting rituals involving a corpse" (118).

According to Myerhoff, a ritual occasion—specifically, a funeral—suggests a series of contradictions. There is always some type of dialectic at work; a public ritual always involves opposites, both for an individual and for the participating community. Certainly our study of film rituals so far would bear this out because film rituals represent "opposites together."

As we have explored the ways in which Hollywood has portrayed children's rituals and then weddings celebrations, we have discovered that these screen rituals correspond to Myerhoff's definition clearly. Birthday parties can be both celebratory and sad; graduations can be both hopeful and empty, and weddings can be beautiful and horrible. Funerals, the final traditional ritual occasion represented in our study, also seem to be characterized by unlike elements.

Like the other ritual occasions, funerals always involve the seemingly contradictory: personal and public, traditional and improvised, simple and complex, dead and living. Again, we can turn to anthropology to help us put into perspective the complications of the funeral rite. Myerhoff explains that most funerals involve at least two kinds of rites, those that acknowledge the dead, and others that acknowledge the living. "Rites of separation may be expected to be predominant in funerary ritual, but most often there will also be some ceremony to separate the dying from the living and to announce the transitional phase between life and death" (116). Like the god Janus, funerary rites always have two faces.

Film funerals are double-faced rituals as well. They almost always include at least two conflicting or clashing narrative perspectives. They are always a study in opposites and sites of inherent tension and conflict. This may explain why, of the traditional rituals of American and Western culture, funerals, like weddings, are so prominent in film. Like weddings, funerals are central ritual occasions in our social matrix; firmly founded in religious traditions, funerals, like baptisms and weddings, look beyond the mundane social necessities and toward the transcendent. Because of their richness, complexity, and dramatic tension, funerals, burials and wakes have become staples of American film, challenging, if not surpassing weddings in terms of frequency as core filmic scenes. Hollywood has used the inherent drama of burying the dead and filming the burying of the dead since before Griffith's *Birth of a Nation* in 1915.[1]

The Wind, a 1928 silent film starring Lillian Gish, offers us an early example of the power of a burial scene. Set in the desert country of California, the film follows Gish as she moves from the East Coast and tries to adjust to a lonely and hard life as the wife of a rough homestead rancher. During one scene, while her husband is away, she resists attack in her house by a loutish farmhand by shooting him to death with her husband's shotgun.

She struggles to drag his body outside, and we watch as she digs a shallow grave in the blowing sand.

As the wind howls around her, she tries to bury the dead man's body in the sand, and she then stumbles back into the house, where she watches the new grave from the window. The camera pans back and forth from Gish's horrified face to the burial site, and we watch as the wind begins to blow off the top of the grave, exposing the man's hands, feet, and finally, his face. By the end of the sequence, his body is almost fully exposed, and we again watch Gish's terror as she realizes that she cannot hide, nor bury, her crime.

The Wind is an early example of how powerful burying the dead can be in film, both visually and symbolically, and also an example of how filmmakers have used the landscape of the American West as burial sites. The genre of American Westerns has always represented funerals and burials as staple scenes, often used to remind us, as does this sequence in *The Wind,* that burying the dead in the desert, mountains, or plains is a necessary housekeeping task, but is never easy. The living must move quickly when burying the dead in Westerns, but the landscape does not yield readily to the human ritual of burying the dead, and the trappings of a religious rite are either missing from these scenes, or are rudimentary at best.

As Gish does, other characters in other Westerns try to bury their dead for multiple reasons: to hide the bodies, to respond hastily to some religious notion of a burial, and to protect the dead from wild predators by burying them on the spot. In Westerns, these scenes show us the most basic elements of the act of burying the dead; there is no time to wait for the trappings of the ritual occasion of a funeral where there is little civilization.

In those Westerns where we do watch a community of mourners gathered for a burial, we come to distinguish brave Christian pioneers or brave Christian soldiers by watching the makeshift religious services held for them. We are used to scenes of a small group of people gathered around a pile of rocks and a wooden cross, with either Western plains or mountains as their background. In these Westerns, funerals remind us that we are in uncivilized territory where the dead must be buried without delay; makeshift cemeteries show up in the West on wagon trails (*Westward the Women*, 1951), in the mountains (*Jeremiah Johnson,* 1972), or in the desert of *The Wind.*

These scenes also help us understand with whom we ought to sympathize. We understand, most often, that the bad guys are the murderers, and the good guys are the ones providing the makeshift burials. Western funeral scenes are often sad and sentimental, begging the audience to feel pity for those involved: those characters in attendance at the burials are isolated on the landscape; the dead are most likely victims of violence, and the music and religious services are makeshift, homespun, and forlorn.[2]

John Ford's epic Western trilogy of cavalry films, *Fort Apache* (1948), *She Wore A Yellow Ribbon* (1949), and *Rio Grande* (1950) all include significant scenes of burials and funerals. Two other of Ford's Westerns, both starring John Wayne, give us our best examples of how burials and funerals in film—Western or otherwise—tell us a great deal about the importance of this ritual occasion. In *The Three Godfathers* (1949) and *The Searchers* (1956), we come to understand that burying the dead becomes an important task for the living characters in the movies. These films become a gauge to how funerals function in other film genres as well.

In *The Three Godfathers* (1948), Robert Hightower (John Wayne) and his fellow bandits Bill Kearney (Harry Carey, Jr.) and Pedro (Pedro Armendariz) come across a lone covered wagon as they are riding through the Arizona desert. Inside the wagon lies a dying woman (Mildred Natwick) with her newborn son in her arms. Before she dies, she asks Bob, Bill and Pedro to become "godfathers" to her baby and to watch over him. Their first obligation to their new godson is to bury his mother.

We watch the three bandits dig a grave on a hilltop, and the next shot is of a wooden cross that has been laid lengthwise on top of the new grave. We see the three godfathers take their hats off and gather around the grave. Bob gives a nod to Bill, who begins singing "Shall We Gather at the River." Bob and Pedro do their best to mouth the words to this hymn for a moment, but they soon make clear that they do not know the words. When Bill reaches the final line of the first stanza, he hesitates. "That all, kid?" growls Bob. "Them's all the words I know, Bob," he replies. "Amen," retorts Bob, as he quickly puts his hat back on. The three men hurry silently down the hill, their task completed. This hastily crafted funeral, with its hand-dug grave, half-sung Christian hymn, and a nod from Bob, has ended.

The funeral in *The Searchers* shares many characteristics with that in *The Three Godfathers*. Shortly after Civil War veteran Ethan Edwards (John Wayne) returns to the Texas ranch of his brother Aaron, Aaron and most of his family are massacred by Comanches. Before Ethan can start searching for Aaron's two daughters, whom he presumes to be captives of the Comanches, he and the Edwards' neighbors hold a short funeral for the massacred family. We see a shot of three wooden crosses, and we hear dissonant sounds from this funeral rite: the mourners sing "Shall We Gather By the River," while the preacher reads aloud from the Bible, over which we hear Ethan's angry voice: "Put an "amen" to it! There's no more time for praying! Amen!" With that command, the funeral ends as Edwards and his men hurry down the side of the hill toward their waiting horses, and in search of the two Edwards girls.

In these two Ford Westerns, the funerals are curt affairs with little more than a light overlay of religiosity. The symbols of Christianity appear briefly, and are interrupted by the immediate needs of the living (in both films represented by the John Wayne character) who must bury the dead, say or sing a few respectful words by rote, and then quickly move on. The funerals serve as thinly veiled religious rites which, in American Westerns, are more secular in nature than sacred. For the audience, the rites of the funeral are so brief and mundane that we know that mourning the dead is not the point. Our allegiance is with the living characters, and any community of mourners on screen becomes merely background to us.

If, as Myerhoff explains, funeral rites serve both to acknowledge the dead and to reaffirm the living, then these

Westerns offer us a paradigm of how funerals function in film. The rites which separate the dead from the living are short—sometimes interrupted—affairs, and the needs of the living community are privileged. However, on film, a sense of "community" in funeral scenes is problematic. When we watch the rites in *The Three Godfathers* and *The Searchers,* we rarely see the mourners, whether they be three outlaws or a small group of Texas ranchers, achieve any sense of community or spiritual relief during these scenes. Bob, Bill and Pedro, now saddled with a newborn infant, must move on quickly to outwit the law in *The Three Godfathers;* Ethan Edwards must search the Texas landscape for his two nieces in *The Searchers*. There is no time for mourning.

Funerals represent the ultimate life passage, and as such, ought to provide the most powerful and sacred sense of community. However, on film, they do the opposite: funerals in American films, Western or otherwise, become not sites of communal grieving and profound sanctity, but sites of isolation, complication, and alienation for the living characters. Indeed, funerals in films rarely bring characters together, or offer any sense of the sacred for audiences. Instead, they most often remind us that funerals are merely ritual occasions, devoid of spiritual transcendence or genuine grief.

Like Westerns, combat films tend to present burials as simple, expedient ceremonies conducted in the urgency of the moment. In *Battleground* (1949), the members of the patrol return to find their comrade dead beneath the overturned jeep where they had left him during an artillery barrage. They pause for a moment, invert his rifle in the snow, and hang a helmet on the rifle butt. In war films the helmet and the rifle, like the make-shift cross of the Western, serve both as a marker and an icon for the fallen. Indeed, in *Steel Helmet* (1951), that icon comes to stand for all who have died in the flow of war.

In moments of respite, there may be time for a short, but moving ceremony. In *Action in the North Atlantic* (1943), Humphrey Bogart has time for a few words about his fallen comrades before they are buried at sea. In *Sands of Iwo Jima*

(1949), the pause that leads to Striker's death also gives his unit a few minutes to grieve for the man (by reading his letter to his son) before they get back into the war.

In most combat films, those who die in the heat of battle rarely get more than a moment's acknowledgment from their buddies. In some ways, that pause, and recognition of loss, while not a ritual, is purer and less muddled than the traditional military funeral.

Also like Westerns, war movies also pull our heartstrings by showing us funeral scenes which seem formulaic in the same way that Westerns are. Military funerals, at home or abroad, include "Taps" and a folded American flag. Often we watch grieving widows and families, sitting in chairs as they watch a flag-clad coffin, receiving flags from color guards. These scenes are so numerous in American film that audiences have come to understand the symbols of military funerals intimately, whether we have ever experienced a military funeral or not. When we watch military funerals, we are also reminded that funeral rites offer us little sense of communal sorrow or sanctity, but instead signal some kind of conflict, dread, or pain for the living mourners.[3]

The symbols and signs associated with military funerals are especially significant in the American production *The Right Stuff* (1983), a film about the earliest years of the NASA/Mercury space program. The scene of a military funeral that opens the film is our most valuable link to the many story lines of this long, complicated narrative. The opening sequence shows us a test-pilot crashing into the California desert outside of Edwards Air Force base. Next, we watch a young woman in bed, startled awake by a bad dream, only to be startled once again by a grim-looking "man in black" who walks slowly toward her front door. We then see a small military funeral out on the desert, where this same grim man sings the Air Force Hymn, and the color guard gives a folded flag to this young widow.

Before any dialogue, any action, or any more flying occurs in *The Right Stuff*, we have watched the burial of an anonymous pilot, whose funeral service will become increasingly important to us as we move through the years toward the film's climactic scenes of the Mercury astronauts' flights in the early 1960s. We will see the grim "man in black" several more times in the movie, most often in scenes where Chuck Yeager (Sam Shepard), the cowboy test-pilot who embodies the Right Stuff, tries to break speed records over Edwards. Near the end of the film, the man in black stands next to the Mercury launch pad when Alan Shepard (Scott Glenn) sits atop Mercury One, waiting to "light this candle" and blast off. The image of this angel of death, who says almost nothing in the film, serves as a quite obvious reminder throughout the film of the earlier test-pilots who tried to light the candle.

We have even more reminders of death and funerals in *The Right Stuff* to help us with the narrative of this movie. Early in the film, we learn that the desert hangout for pilots at Edwards is a rough-looking inn, run by a rough-looking woman named "Pancho." Pancho keeps bar, and on the wall behind her bar are framed pictures of pilots. When one patron asks her how a pilot gets his picture on the wall, Pancho tells her that "he has to die." Throughout the film, the wall behind Pancho's bar becomes another funerary symbol for us, as we watch the test-pilots become astronauts. Near the end of the film, we see a scene in which Pancho's inn burns to the ground. The camera closes in on the frames on the wall as they burn and wither. For the audience, this wall, like the man in black, becomes an easy gauge to our understanding of honor, time, and death in *The Right Stuff*.

Like most other American films which include scenes of funerals and burials, *The Right Stuff* offers us a paradox, a series of opposites, where we see symbols of both death and life. During the early burial scene of the anonymous pilot, we watch his casket lowered into the ground at the same time that we are introduced to one of his mourners, ace pilot Chuck Yeager. Also, Pancho's bar represents both a mausoleum and a tavern—in the same scene where Pancho nails another framed pilot onto the wall behind the bar, we also see couples laughing and dancing on the other side of the bar.

Like the funeral symbols in *The Right Stuff,* funerals in other Hollywood movies serve not so much as conclusions, but as beginnings. Unlike wedding scenes, which conclude scores of movies, funerals are rarely used as final scenes in films. In fact, there are only a few popular films which allow the audiences to grieve at the end of the films. *Chariots of Fire* (1981) opens with a scene of the funeral of runner Harold Abrahams, moves quickly to the flashback narrative of Abrahams and the other British runners who won gold medals at the 1924 Olympics, and concludes as it began, with a scene of a luminous ritual occasion and communal hymn at Abrahams' funeral. *The Group* (1966) concludes with the elaborate funeral and burial of one of the Vassar graduates, Kay (Joanna Pettet), a character whose death we are allowed to mourn with her friends. *The Deer Hunter* (1978) ends with a series of funeral scenes, allowing the audience to experience the Ukrainian ceremony and the genuine sorrow along with the people who loved Vietnam War victim Nick (Christopher Walken).

However, concluding funerals in the movies are rare. Most funerals on film are about the living as much or more than about the dead; these ritual occasions, whether they are scenes on a wilderness landscape or in a cathedral, tell us that life goes on. What Hollywood productions use funeral rituals to tell us about is precisely *how* life goes on, and most often, life beyond a funeral in a Hollywood production is fraught with problems.

In the same way that weddings of characters we do not know allow us to focus on other characters and plot complications in wedding scenes, most movies use the sacred symbols of death and mourning to help an audience understand that funeral and burial rites are about living characters. Certainly, any movie detective, from Sam Spade in *The Maltese Falcon* (1941) to Philip Marlowe in *Murder, My Sweet* (1944) to Easy Rawlins in *Devil in a Blue Dress* (1995), knows that the real stories begin at funerals, where murderers often show up and the mysteries of crimes begin to unravel. The literary antecedents of these classic detective films also reflect this use of funerals: a narrative begins when someone dies.[4]

Movie funerals in Westerns, military, or crime films are easy to predict and to understand because they are part of a mosaic of standard Hollywood devices that represent institutional funerals.[5] Civilian funerals in Hollywood films also conform to certain patterns, some of which correspond directly to those of these specific genre-based rituals. Funerals in the movies always reflect the "double-faced" nature of funerary rituals —they always suggest death and life, sorrow and consolation, isolation and community. Movie funerals also function in ways that other rituals do in American films: they show us, through the religious symbols and community traditions they project, the opposite of what these symbols should represent. Most often when we watch a film funeral, where we should be allowed to experience grief, loss, and some sense of communal love, we instead watch characters experience confusion and isolation from the grieving process. No matter what the genre—comedy, drama, melodrama—a movie that shows us a funeral rarely allows us to grieve; this most sacred and final of all ritual occasions rarely offers us consolation, community, or peace.

There are many American films that are developed around the funeral of some character we do not ever know, but whose death has brought together characters we come to care about during the movie. *The Bad and the Beautiful* (1952), a Hollywood film about Hollywood, is structured as a series of flashbacks about bad boy producer Jonathan Shields (Kirk Douglas). We know he has many enemies before we actually see him, and when we do finally see him in the first flashback, we see him standing among mourners at a lavish Beverly Hills funeral, where we find out that he has hired extras to "act like mourners" for a dead film producer he hates. In Sidney Lumet's *Bye Bye Braverman* (1968), we never see Braverman, but instead watch a group of his friends drive around New York City looking for his funeral. And in *The Big Chill* (1983), we come to know a group of old college friends who have gathered to mourn the suicide death of their friend, Alex, whose funeral becomes our first glimpse into the world of these 1960s-turned-1980s young professionals. We never see more than Alex's corpse being groomed in the opening credits of the film, but we get to know his friends intimately, beginning at his funeral, where one of them plays an organ rendition of the Rolling Stones' "You Can't Always Get What You Want."

Other movies open with scenes of funerals of parents, which, like the opening scenes of *Hamlet* or a good Victorian novel, leave parentless children who must survive by their own wits. *Doctor Zhivago* (1965) begins with a very elaborate sequence in which the child Yuri Zhivago throws dirt into his mother's grave during an Orthodox funeral service. Out on the Texas prairie, Addie (Tatum O'Neal) stands sadly by her mother's grave until Moses Pray (Ryan O'Neal) reluctantly consents to take her to Missouri in *Paper Moon* (1973). Celie (Desreta Jackson), in her first letter to God, tells of how her mama died "cause her heart done broke" as she and her sister walk behind a wagon carrying her mother's casket in *The Color Purple* (1985). And brothers Raymond (Dustin Hoffman) and Charlie (Tom Cruise) meet for the first time at their father's funeral in *Rain Man* (1988).

We expect scenes of funerals to show up in films of high drama or in melodrama, in the same way that we understand the plethora of funerals in Westerns and war films. Yet, in American cinema, where we might least expect to see a variety of funeral rituals is precisely where they seem to show up the most: in comedies. Because they most often suggest the opposite of what they represent in American culture, in Hollywood comedies, funerals have long been part of a tradition of laughter, used to delight us more that to sadden us, or used to promote sight gags or running jokes involving not the dead, but the living.

Both *The Loved One* (1965) and *Harold and Maude* (1971) are Hollywood productions in which death, funerals, and burials are crucial to plot, character, and narrative; these movies are about funerals. They were both produced in the Hollywood environment of the 1960s, and they both reflect the skepticism toward institutions and toward traditional values which characterized much of American, and Western culture of the Vietnam era. *The Loved One,* directed by Tony Richardson and based on the Evelyn Waugh novel, was a truly experimental (and funny) film which initially suffered poor critical reviews because it was thought to be too dark. Released during the height of the "cultural revolution," *The Loved One* offered the first significant Hollywood parody of the funeral industry and of the institutional industries of death: the church, the family, the law.

By the time *Harold and Maude* was released in 1971, the criticisms towards *The Loved One* were moot; *Harold and Maude* became a cult classic, especially with young Americans, whose need to shake institutional foundations was projected aptly by mainstream Hollywood. Harold, a rich, neglected twenty-year-old, spends his time staging suicides for his preoccupied mother, driving around in his hearse, and attending funerals and burials of people he does not know. Early in the film his mother sends him to see a psychiatrist, who asks him what he does with his time. "I go to funerals," Harold replies.

As Harold gets to know Maude, a 79-year-old eccentric, and as we get to know them both, we might begin to notice that Harold's staged suicides and funeral visits become fewer and fewer. Near the end of the film, Harold goes to Maude's ramshackle home to celebrate her eightieth birthday, and she informs him that she has taken poison capsules to bring on her own death. In the final sequence of the film, Harold, formerly an obsessive suicide brat, tries desperately—and unsuccessfully— to save Maude's life.

The great irony of *Harold and Maude* is that this film about death wishes and the imprisonment of the human spirit within traditional institutional shackles, instead becomes a movie where being alive is affirmed and celebrated. *Harold and Maude* may be considered a "dark comedy," but it is the funeral experience that allows an audience to understand Harold's growth and enlightenment. However, we know that Harold's newfound growth has come at a heavy price. When Harold finally celebrates Maude's life at the end of the film, he does so by staging his own private funeral rite for Maude, as he stands alone, singing "their" song while he cries. He has learned a great deal from Maude, who showed him the attention he found from no one else in his life. However, his funeral celebration makes very clear to us that Harold is once again alone, grieving for Maude in isolation.

Since *The Loved One* and *Harold and Maude,* many American films that bill themselves as comedies have used funerals and burials as sites for comic relief. Couples meet and fall in love because of funeral services: in *Only the Lonely* (1991), a young police officer (John Candy) meets his love (Ally Sheedy) in her father's funeral home, where she is experimenting with makeup on a corpse. In *Used People* (1992), Pearl (Shirley MacLaine) includes an uninvited guest (Marcello Mastroianni) into her home during her husband's funeral reception, and he promptly asks her out to dinner. And in *Private Benjamin* (1980), poor Judy Benjamin, lying on her bed after the funeral of a husband who died on their wedding night, is comforted by an elderly aunt who asks Judy what her husband's last words were. "I'm coming," Judy sobs, and the scene changes immediately, denying us a look at the shock on the mourning aunt's face, but allowing us the wicked delight nevertheless.

Some American movies use funeral homes or family deaths as the basis for their comedy: perpetual widow Louisa Foster (Shirley MacLaine) buries six wealthy husbands before she finally marries a poor man in *What a Way to Go!* (1964). An entire extended family fights over the patriarch's estate in *Passed Away* (1993), and a group of Washington elites discuss the future presidential campaign for idiot savant Chance the Gardner (Peter Sellers) in *Being There* (1979) while they carry a casket into a mausoleum. In perhaps the most famous of all funny funeral scenes in an American film, soldiers in a Korean MASH unit stage a "last supper" for suicidal Painless the Dentist, complete with a musical tribute, "Suicide Is Painless," in Robert Altman's 1970 production of *M*A*S*H.*

American audiences have become used to the rituals of death as part of comedy since the silent era, and corpses, caskets, funerals, and burials have been a staple of the talkies as well (Roland Young stages and attends his own funeral in the 1933 production of *His Double Life,* and Monty Woolley does the same in the 1943 remake, *Holy Matrimony*). In these comedies, often billed as "slapstick," the tension associated with death and dying is relieved by sight gags which use the symbols of the funeral ritual, and by periodic outbursts of laughter. Ironically, it is in these comedies which use death as a means to laughter, that we are most likely to find scenes where characters are genuinely sad. In fact, in some scenes in Hollywood productions billed as comedies, the audience comes closest to experiencing grief with the characters.

In *The Big Chill,* the funeral and burial for Alex ends, and the mourners gather for a reception at the home of Harold (Kevin Kline) and Sarah (Glenn Close), where, as we have learned, Alex committed suicide. Friend and fellow mourner Karen (JoBeth Williams) compliments Sarah on how lovely the reception is. Sarah quips without thinking, "Yeah, we put on a great funeral here . . . we give first preference to people who kill themselves in one of our bathrooms." Karen looks away from Sarah, embarrassed. "That was a terrible thing to say," Sarah says to Karen quietly, after an uncomfortable silence.

Until this point, Sarah and the other mourning friends have been joking to each other with such regularity that we might have doubted their sincerity. With this comment by Sarah, who feels she has crossed the line between acceptable glibness and inappropriate, unfunny commentary on her friend's death, we begin to understand that the jokes among these friends are their way of coping with their shock and loss. Laughing about death, laughing about the funeral rite and the process of grief, are what allow these friends to find their sense of community. As Sarah has pointed out to us, Alex's death in her bathroom is not funny. It is so awful that she has no words beyond the mundane with which to express her sorrow.

My Girl (1991) is another good example of a Hollywood film, originally billed as a family comedy, which uses the environment of a funeral home to help us understand the power of grief and loss to the living characters. Vada (Anna Chlumsky) is a bright eleven-year-old girl whose mother died when Vada was born, and who has been raised by her funeral-director father (Dan Ackroyd). They live above the funeral home, and Vada often "baby sits" for her grandmother in one room of the house while her father directs a funeral in another room.

Vada, who is obsessed with the death of her mother and intrigued by the corpses her father prepares in their basement, seems oblivious to the grief displayed by mourners in her father's funeral home; she seems annoyed by the intrusion into her life of the funeral process in her home. About halfway through the movie, however, Vada's best friend, Thomas Jay (Macauley Culkin) dies from an extreme reaction to bee stings, and Vada must confront not just the ritual occasion of the funeral, but her own understanding of death and grief.

Until this point, the funeral scenes in the film have all been used for comic purposes—to show Grandma's senility as she interrupts a funeral singing "Ten Cents a Dance," for instance—or to allow us to become aware of Vada's obsession with the concept of death. However, when Thomas Jay's funeral begins in the funeral parlor of her house, Vada is too grief-stricken to attend. She sits alone on the stairs, listening to the service. Finally, she peeks in, and despondent, interrupts the service and walks up to the open casket, crying that Thomas Jay ought to be wearing his glasses. If we have not understood what Vada struggles through here, we now understand. Funerals no longer represent the profession of her father, or the rituals of other people to Vada. We learn with Vada that funerals mean pain, that death means sorrow, loss, and injustice. Vada can now, for the first time, transcend her mundane adolescent world and learn to grieve for those she has lost.

My Girl can be categorized in any number of ways, as a coming-of-age film, as a family drama, as a dark comedy. How we categorize the movie becomes irrelevant at some point, however, in the same way that Vada's childish obsession with death becomes irrelevant when her friend dies. We understand from watching the various funeral symbols and rituals of the film that for Vada, knowing how funerals are prepared does not prepare her for the loss of someone she loves. Losing Thomas Jay allows her to begin to understand the loss of her mother and the love of her father, and we watch Vada mature by the end of the movie because of her changing responses to the funerals around her.

Hollywood comedy represents that genre of drama which offers us visions of the trivial and the serendipitous. Comedies provide the movie sites where funerals become most meaningful, where these sacred ritual occasions actually allow us the relief of mourning. *The Big Chill* and *My Girl* are two good examples of how film can show us what happens when our day-to-day lives are violated by death. Comedies especially have the power to project what happens to people when those trivial details of their lives are interrupted by the sudden loss of people they love. Funerals in comedies, with their sight gags, wisecracks, and blunders, allow us to understand that life is fragile, that people are vulnerable, and that the death of loved ones hurts us in unspeakable ways, making us behave in peculiar ways.

Through the years, Hollywood has provided us with many examples of funerals (like the very sad one for Thomas Jay in *My Girl*) which serve to help living characters come to terms with their own lives, and which suggest to the audience the profound sense of the loneliness in the grieving process. The 1934 production of *Imitation of Life,* and the remake in 1959, both include elaborate funeral services which become vivid examples of how funeral rituals give us both the public drama of the ritual occasion and the private agony of grief. Filmed almost exactly alike, these two funeral processions mark the death of a beloved character, Delilah (Louise Beavers) in the 1934 production, who becomes Annie (Juanita Moore) in the 1959 film.

The 1959 production of *Imitation of Life* has been the subject of several feminist readings, and the final funeral scene has been the site of much scholarly discussion.[6] The film, directed by Douglas Sirk, follows the careers of two single working mothers in New York, one white (Lana Turner as Lora), and one black (Moore). Lora, an aspiring actress who struggles to make a living for herself and her young daughter Susie, reluctantly consents to take in Annie and her daughter, light-skinned Sara Jane. The four of them become a "family," where Lora, ambitious and driven to become an actress, works outside the home and Annie works in the home as housekeeper, secretary, and mother to the girls.

Wakes, Funerals, and Burials · 81

As the years go by, we watch two major story lines develop: the rise of Lora's career at the expense of her relationship with her lonely and neglected daughter, and the struggles of Annie's daughter Sara Jane to live as a young black woman who can pass for white. Sara Jane attempts to pass several times, telling her mother to leave her alone. Sara Jane runs away from home; shortly thereafter, Annie becomes ill and dies. The final scenes in the movie show us what happens to this "family" by showing us Annie's funeral.

As film scholar Jackie Byars points out, "Annie's death ruptures the narrative, providing a motivation for dramatic changes and enabling a sad but 'happy' ending" (252). Indeed, the film offers us a number of readings of these final funeral scenes. The funeral service takes place in a black church where Mahalia Jackson, in a cameo appearance, sings, and the procession outside is appointed by an all-black color guard. Just as Annie's coffin is being loaded onto an elaborately decorated white horse-drawn-carriage, Sara Jane runs from the crowd of onlookers to embrace the coffin, and is pulled away into a waiting limousine by Lora. The final shots of the movie show us Lora, with Sara Jane's head on her shoulder and Susie's hand in her hand, comforting both daughters, while her long-time suitor Steve (John Gavin) watches them from the opposite seat.

Byars suggests that in some sense, Lora "becomes at least momentarily a surrogate mother to Sara Jane," but even this position of the "family" is tentative because Steve has been interjected into this family scene and sits across from the grieving family of women, ready to displace all of their positions as Father and Husband. As Byars points out, the "happy ending" of the film is quite tenuous because Steve's "gaze and his physical separation from the group of women" places him at an uncomfortable distance from Lora, Susie, and Sara Jane; thus "the unity of the family is placed in question" (258).

Annie's funeral serves, says Byars, as a symbol of the imitation of life represented in the narrative: "the excessive opulence of the funeral, the opulence of the funeral procession, and the heightened drama of Sara Jane's return . . . call attention to the artificiality of happy endings" (257). Although Sara Jane has returned, her mother is dead, and she is still a young black girl at the mercy of a white family, now symbolically headed by a new patriarchal figure. The fantastic funeral display, "where glitter and glamour accompany the solemn ritual of humble people," serves to remind us that in fact, there is little opulence in the life of a black female in America in 1959. Annie's death is that of a martyr, and Sara Jane's future as a member of her family is not reconciled, but remains tenuous (256).

For Sara Jane, her mother's death should represent her release from the one facet of her life that forced her to be a black woman: her mother. Yet this funeral does not seem to be a happy ending to the film; as director Sirk commented, "You don't believe the happy end, and you're not supposed to" (qtd. in Byars 257). Like so many film funerals, this one from *Imitation of Life* forces us to consider the double-faced quality of the funeral ritual: we may feel grief, anger, relief, and fear, all at the same time. What we probably will not feel at the conclusion of this movie, however, is any sense of resolution or community.

Imitation of Life offers us an example of one of the most complicated film funerals in American cinema, and again reinforces a characteristic that film funerals share with other film rituals: they signal to an audience the opposite of what we expect. Funerals are especially complicated on film because they can, like *Imitation of Life,* suggest multiple responses, none of which may correspond to an actual death. As Myerhoff has pointed out, the separation rituals of funerals are for a living community of mourners, and yet on film, they always suggest the loneliness and private journeys of characters who must fight their way through the elaborate maze of a public ritual occasion to discover their own sense of grief.

Whether a funeral shows up in a comedy, a musical like *Oklahoma!* or *Paint Your Wagon* (1969), or in a Hitchcock film or a melodrama, when we see funeral rituals in American movies, we are always confronted with a complicated narrative of life in death. In the same way that scenes of weddings tell us little about love, or juvenile birthday party scenes tell us little about the joys of childhood, burial rites in the movies tell us little about grieving. Film funerals show us the elaborate symbols of how people say goodbye to the dead, and how the living, who ought to use the occasions to cleave to each other, instead cope with grief in their own private ways. Westerns allow us to see how thin the veneer of the funeral ritual is, as we watch isolated mourners pay lip service to religious symbols on the empty landscape; war movies allow us to see how traditional military symbols and rites do not comfort the living; comedies offer us sudden, nervous laughter and pratfalls amid tears.

Movie funerals merely suggest the profound ways in which sorrow and loss will affect the living. When Coalhouse Walker's (Howard Rollins) fiancee is beaten to death in *Ragtime,* he provides her with a lavish funeral, buries her in her wedding gown, and then plans a vigilante attack on the white community that ensures that he, too, will die. When Beth McColley's (Jessica Lange) husband dies in an electrical accident in *Men Don't Leave* (1989), she moves with her two sons to Baltimore and struggles through a nervous breakdown before she can turn her loss into something of value. When Charles Foster Kane dies, the newsreel footage of his lavish funeral prompts a young journalist to search for answers about this enigmatic life. As we come along on the journey that is *Citizen Kane* (1941), what we learn about the late Mr. Kane becomes a long spiral of tragedies, but his death is not one of them.

Funerals in American movies allow us to understand that the traditional ritual occasions we use to mark the deaths of loved ones are public displays that can never provide relief from our feelings of loss, which are ultimately private and personal. Funerals on film rarely allow either characters or audience the chance to grieve. When Ethan Edwards tells us in *The Searchers,* "there's no more time for praying!" he is articulating precisely how funeral rites function in American film. Funerals are public displays which suggest that grief, like love, joy, or fear, has its own life, away from the burial site or the church, and that our sense of loss is grounded in solitude, not in community.

Hollywood's projections of ritual funerary occasions point out to us that public rituals are not where we will see genuine human sorrow portrayed for us on a screen. And, although we always mourn characters we have come to love—the stalwart immigrant grandmother (Joan Plowright) in *Avalon* (1990), the scrappy GI (Frank Sinatra) in *From Here to Eternity* (1953), the hard-working Vassar grad Kay in *The Group,* the war-torn Vietnam veteran Nick (Christopher Walken) in *The Deer Hunter*—like the people who bury these characters, we will have to find our own ways of coping with their deaths.

Of all the examples of funeral rites in Hollywood productions, Nick's funeral in *The Deer Hunter* may best symbolize the heart of the funeral experience in American film. We hear the sad, beautiful strains of the traditional Ukrainian funeral music, and we see a shot of the cathedral spires. We watch Nick's hometown buddies and the women who loved him sit through the long, elaborate orthodox funeral ceremony, and we see them carrying his casket slowly to the waiting hearse, where his comrade Mike, dressed in his formal military attire, lays his hand on the casket in a farewell gesture. The final scene of the movie takes place just after the burial, as Nick's friends, sitting in their favorite local tavern, raise their glasses in a toast and sing to Nick's memory. They have chosen a particularly poignant—and ironic—song: "God Bless America." As they sing, we see close-ups of their individual faces; they are all struggling to sing while they cry.

This, the final scene of a heartbreaking epic, is a quiet moment, in which friends together yet alone, sing and cry simultaneously. It reminds us, sadly enough, that funerals in Hollywood movies reflect the double-edged nature of this ritual occasion: although characters come together to mourn the dead, the ritual occasion of the funeral offers not a sense of community, but the sadness of grieving alone. How characters in Hollywood movies transcend the heavy and dark symbols of their ritual occasions, how they find ways to feel illuminated by genuine joy, love, or sorrow, has little to do with their ritual occasions.

5

LUMINOUS MOMENTS IN HOLLYWOOD FILMS

The ritual occasions of American movies represent moments where we meet ourselves and where we lose ourselves, because the rituals and rites we watch on screen look both familiar and foreign. As we have seen, the symbols of American movie rituals—mortar boards, crucifixes, birthday cakes, white veils, coffins—are nearly always counterbalanced in the movies by dialog, camera shots, or music which betray or belie the drama of the moment. When we watch scenes of ritual, we understand the ritual of the culture, yet we may not always be prepared for the contradictions in what we are watching—for instance, that graduation in *St. Elmo's Fire* (1985) leads to disappointment, that marriage in *The Deer Hunter* signals heartbreak, that death in *Harold and Maude* makes life worth living.

The ritual occasions of the real world from which these cinematic scenes are drawn are rarely associated with surprise; we all know what to expect when we attend weddings, for instance, or we remember too well the confusion and pain of planning a funeral. Rituals in the movies, however, are predictable only because of their unpredictable nature. Watching ritual occasions in the movies may help us understand many things—the traditions of a culture, the circumstances of characters, the complications of plot—but rarely do these scenes help us find resolution or clarity. Ritual scenes, whether of infant baptism or funerals, show us a variety of emotions and human behaviors which reflect the tangled drama of rituals themselves: loneliness, fear, sorrow, lust, disappointment, longing. Ritual scenes identify to audiences elements in film that are uneven, jarring, and often confusing.

What ritual occasions on film rarely identify for us are the impetus for these occasions. Because the performers of the ritual dramas we see on film are so often not the characters who most interest us, nor their stories more than devices, we usually do not need to see more than the surface ritual acts of their lives. For instance, when the sister of Maerose (Anjelica Huston) marries in the first scene of *Prizzi's Honor,* we don't care much about the details of her sister's courtship, but we care very much about other relationships suggested to us by the camera. That this film opens with the marriage ritual of people who are not important to us identifies it as a good example of how Hollywood films use ritual: a love story of people we do care about begins by portraying a marriage between a couple about whom we do not care.

Hollywood films most often do not use scenes of ritual occasions or rites—or, for that matter, scenes of religious or national holidays—to tell us about the love, friendship, or spiritual bonds among characters with whom we are most closely allied during films. In the movies, ritual occasions are the suggestive symbols for those bonds, which, as has been seen, are most often characterized by emotions in opposition to the symbols they represent.

If Hollywood films use rituals as devices where viewers do not invest much into the rituals, and if the rituals do not tell us much about the characters we do invest in, just where are the points in these films where the audience does become engaged in the characters' lives, in the plots, in the films? Where in these movies, if not in the scenes of ritual, do we find the motivations, depths, bonds, among characters? Where do we find the love, joy, grief, which lead these characters and their audiences to experience ritual occasions at all?

One of the best ways to begin to answer this question is to return to the start of this study of American film rituals: to Michael Corleone's memory in *Godfather II* of his father's birthday party on December 7, 1941. As the four grown children of Vito Corleone sit around the dining room table waiting to surprise their absent father on his birthday, Michael delivers a surprise of his own to his siblings: he has joined the Marines. Tom and Sonny are aghast and dismayed, and they both warn Michael that his father will be horrified. "Break your father's heart on his birthday," Sonny whines, and Tom agrees, adding, "Mikey, he has high hopes for you."

The flashback ends when the family leaves Michael alone at the table while they all move off screen to welcome their father, and Michael sits brooding, waiting. He sits in much the same position that he sits during the final scene in Tahoe, when he is also alone and brooding, knowing his brother Fredo has just been murdered at his command. As the flashback fades, we might expect Michael of 1941 to fade back into Michael in 1959 Tahoe, but instead we see another image. It is so quick that we might miss it, except for its sharp poignancy.

Michael at the birthday party table melts into a shot of the young Vito Corleone (DeNiro), and we see a glimpse of Vito, holding toddler Michael to wave goodbye from a train window as they leave Sicily. Earlier in the film, we have seen similar scenes: after murdering Fanucci, Vito returns to his tenement steps, takes baby Michael in his arms, and whispers, louder to us than the parade they are watching, "Michael, your father loves you very much."

Coming at the end of Michael's flashback then, is a scene which, like all of the scenes of young Vito, dovetails into Michael's 1959 Tahoe in stunning, alarming ways. The shot of Vito and Michael on the train is not Michael's memory, but ours, at this point, and the double narrative has finally come together in ways that make the two memories one. What we understand because of these two scenes is that no matter what else he did during his lifetime, Michael's father did love him very much. Michael, his only living son in 1959, has fulfilled his father's hopes for him in ways that Vito might not recognize, but which we do. Michael's powerful Family is now his only family, whether his father loved him very much or not.

In his essay on the *Godfather* films, John Yates concludes by acknowledging the power of the father/son parallels and relationship between Vito and Michael and by pointing out that the *Godfather* films, far from providing a nostalgic look at the past, "apologize for nothing in the past, and hide nothing" (203). He continues:

> Nor do they pretend that the past could or should have survived. But they mourn its passing. . . . They mourn a time when personal liberation hadn't locked us all in our own individual cells. They mourn a time when our fathers loved us very much. (203)

The Godfather films, all three of them, are not just movies about the Corleone family and its traditions; they are movies specifically about fathers and their sons, and about the power of love between a father and son. Ironically, this great American epic, used here to identify the ominous power of ritual occasions, is also a significant example of how love shows up in American film. The scenes of love between Michael and his father, between Michael and his son Anthony, between Michael and his nephew Vincent, are scenes of enlightenment for an audience. They are the most luminous moments in the *Godfather* saga; however, they are not scenes of ritual occasions.

These scenes of luminosity in *The Godfather* trilogy are often quiet, private moments when we recognize that Don Corleone and his son love each other. In *The Godfather,* when Michael visits his stricken father in the hospital and maneuvers his father's bed out of the room to save him from assassins, he whispers "I'm with you, Pop." The Don, unable to speak, looks at Michael with tears running down his face. A few scenes later, we see a shot of Fredo, crying quietly, as he sits bedside his father's bed. And, in perhaps the most powerful and touching scene of love in the film, Michael and his father, now retired, discuss plans and make small talk while they sit together in the Don's garden.

Vito: I like to drink wine more than I used to. Anyway, I'm drinking more.
Michael: It's good for you, Pop . . .
Vito: How's your boy?
Michael: He's good.

Vito: You know, he looks more like you every day.
Michael: He's smarter than I am.

This is the final scene between Vito Corleone and Michael, and near the end of their conversation, the Don laments to Michael, "I never wanted this for you. Senator Corleone, Governor Corleone. Just wasn't enough time, Michael." Michael replies with a reassuring "We'll get there, Pop. We'll get there," before his father gives him a tender kiss on the cheek.

There are few scenes in any of the *Godfather* films to match this one in its quiet power, or for its visual beauty. Like so many of the scenes in which the Don interacts with his family, (his graceful dance scene with daughter Connie at her wedding; his final scene in the garden with grandson Anthony) this one takes place outdoors, and seems drenched in light. These are the scenes which most pointedly allow an audience into the Corleone family by lighting up the screen.

There are other such scenes throughout the *Godfather* trilogy, most always scenes of intimacy between fathers and sons. Michael tucks a young Anthony into bed after the confirmation scene, explaining that he has to go away on business to Havana, and Anthony offers to accompany him, telling him "I could help you." In *Godfather III,* after Michael has been hospitalized for acute diabetes, his nephew Vincent shares a small, sweet moment with him at his bedside.

The luminous moments in these films stand in opposition to the ritual moments. While scenes of ritual occasions most often signal impending danger or violence in the Corleone world, these scenes of love and light make the Corleones accessible to us in more basic ways. These sequences where fathers and sons express their care and love for each other are the scenes that make the Corleones human. We can argue, in fact, that in the *Godfather* films, the most "human" of the Corleones is Vito himself, because we see so many scenes where he is engaged in these small moments of his early domestic life in *Godfather II.*

Shots and scenes like these in *The Godfather*—scenes of bedside chats, of parents dancing with children, of private conversations between family members—represent the luminous moments of Hollywood productions, those scenes or camera shots which serve as counterpoint to scenes of ritual occasions. These luminous moments show up in ways that make them seem unselfconscious, in complete contrast to ritual scenes, which always seem self-consciously staged and directed. The moments in an American film where an audience most feels for characters, or understands clearly the drama of the moment, are often to be found in scenes where characters are engaged not in traditional rituals, but in the ritualized behaviors of everyday life, for instance, during bedtime or sickbed scenes, or during scenes of dancing, swimming or bathing.

When Francie's father tucks her into bed on Christmas Eve in *A Tree Grows in Brooklyn,* he kisses her and tells her tenderly that she has "a very bad case of growing up." Later, while Francie tends to her now-widowed mother who is lying in bed in the throes of labor, the two of them have their first real mother-daughter talk. "I didn't want for you to have to grow up so soon," Katie Nolan laments to Francie, in a tone not unlike Vito Corleone's tone when he laments his son's fate at the end of *The Godfather.* Intimate moments between parents and children happen during scenes like these, and for an audience, these private conversations become special enlightening moments, as if we are privy to other people's dreams. When Homer's father helps him, a returning wounded veteran, dress for bed in *The Best Years of Our Lives,* we watch an almost silent scene of love and care as the older man helps his son put on pajamas.

Even in films billed as comedies, luminous moments help us to understand aspects of the films that make characters seem human. In *Sixteen Candles,* Samantha's birthday, the "single worst day" of her life, ends on a poignant note when her father remembers, finally, that the family has forgotten her birthday, and tiptoes downstairs to her bed to tell her. In *Postcards from the Edge* (1990), Suzanne (Meryl Streep), adult daughter of a famous and difficult movie actress (Shirley MacLaine), spends time in the hospital with her mother, who has been admitted after smashing her car into a tree. In the only scene of the film where the two are not fighting, we watch as Suzanne helps her bedridden mother by applying her mother's makeup with care. If only for a moment, they love each other unconditionally, and we get to be there.

We watch characters begin to heal themselves while they help others in many Hollywood productions beyond *Postcards from the Edge*. Celie's life begins to change for the better the day she begins to care for her husband's lover, Shug Avery, in *The Color Purple*. As she bathes and feeds Shug, and as Shug gradually becomes healthier and happier, we see Celie also becoming healthier and happier, as her self-esteem and ability to function outside of her unhappy home grow and improve. And when Beth (Jessica Lange), a widowed mother whose life has become so stressful that she has locked herself in her apartment, is pried out of bed and nursed back to health by her teenage son's older girlfriend (Joan Cusack) in *Men Don't Leave* (1989), we watch the two women come to terms with each other as Beth's health improves.

The scenes in American films where we see love or joy are often subtle, in direct contrast to the often elaborate scenes of ritual. In *Fried Green Tomatoes,* there are several ritual scenes, yet the scenes where we understand the growing love between Idgie (Mary Stuart Masterson) and Ruth (Mary-Louise Parker) are those that take place as they swim together alone. Norma Rae (Sally Field) and Reuben (Ron Liebman) are very different people from two different worlds in *Norma Rae* (1979), who work together tirelessly to unionize garment workers. They have only a few scenes together where we see them learning to like each other. At one point, tired and hot from canvassing door to door, they jump into a pond for a swim. "Reuben, you've got a skinny build," Norma Rae drawls, as she swims toward him. We cannot help but notice, as they swim in this peaceful, sunlit pond, that they are finally friends.

Although dancing is a public ritualized activity, in Hollywood movies, scenes of dancing allow us to watch people having private moments. We see teenage steadies Steve (Ron Howard) and Laurie (Cindy Williams), struggling to seem happy on the night before they part, as they dance alone in the spotlight at a sock hop in *American Graffiti* (1973).[1] There are two wedding scenes in *The Philadelphia Story,* yet where we get a sense of Tracy Lord's vulnerabilities is in a scene where she dances with MacCaulay Connor (James Stewart), the two of them alone on a poolside patio in the dark. And when her adolescent son asks widow Edna (Sally Field) to dance in *Places in the Heart* (1984), she lights up, remembering her husband, and beaming with pride and love for her son.

The scenes in American films where small, ritualized, everyday behaviors and habits lighten the screen for us are many. Like scenes of ritual occasions, these scenes contribute to the film narratives in ways that resist categorization; they appear in films from every genre, from every decade, from many different directors and casts. Without scenes in which we are privy to the private lives and habits of characters, the ritual occasions we watch mean little or nothing; luminous private moments provide an emotional standard by which we understand public ritual occasions and whether they become transformative and transcendent moments. Although the ways in which Hollywood films have portrayed rituals have changed through the decades, the emotional needs of characters—their longings, needs, fear, and joys—remain constant.[2]

And the significance of scenes of ritual occasions, from baptisms through funerals, *has* changed dramatically. Where we once might have expected joy in a wedding or a graduation scene, we now often watch a cliched, predictable scene where something bad will happen. Through the years, American cinema has reflected and projected the larger American cultural changes: ritual occasions, and the institutions from which they derive, are often portrayed with skepticism, cynicism, or a sense of the fatal. Scenes of joy, of triumph, or of fulfillment, most often show up in small, unexpected places in Hollywood productions—most often, but not always.

Especially since 1945, one genre of American film can be characterized as successfully and consistently combining ritual with meaningful transcendence: the sports movie. Just as scenes of traditional ritual occasions in Hollywood films surprise us by offering us the opposite of what we think we are watching, sports films provide us with a like paradox. We find that a story about the limits and ritualized strainings of the human body is never a story about the physical world of an athlete. Sports films, always defined by some institutional constraints or "rules of the game," transcend these constraints and become Hollywood's most consistent celebration of the unlimited striving of the human spirit.[3]

In the strictly formulaic sense, sports are clearly among the most ritualized human activities of our culture. Tightly circumscribed by rules that extend even to matters of dress and language, sporting events are highly formal competitions with large and engaged audiences. Although the outcome of a sporting event is not predetermined, the events themselves have clear ending points that mark the end of the occasion.

Sports not only make familiar conventions clear to us, like the triumph of the underdog (the Cutter bicycle team in *Breaking Away*) and the power of the tough but sensitive coach (Jack Warden in *Heaven Can Wait*), but also suggest the particular importance of some of those conventions as components of true rituals. Although sports films as a group do not typically present themselves or their sports as anything more than spectacles of competition, they do in many ways suggest that sports are not simply secular ritualized activities. At times, sports films become genuine rituals which offer both participants and spectators the kind of cultural nourishment and transcendent awareness of true ritual occasions.

Among the many conventions that regularly appear in the sport film, two are of particular interest because of the ways they suggest that sporting events are not simply safe substitutes for warfare, as some critics have suggested, or simply metaphoric acting out of the kinds of competition central to a capitalist society. These two elements might be called the scene of recognition or awareness, and the mobbing scene.

In the scene of recognition or awareness, our hero (rarely a female), faces his own doubts about his own worthiness as a competitor and/or the worth of the competition itself. Like a neophyte, he is typically counseled by an older and wiser person, and comes to recognize that his self worth, now and in the future, depends on meeting the challenge of the competition.

That this moment of self doubt, followed by recognition and heightened awareness, is related to larger issues than mere personal insecurity, is perhaps nowhere better presented than in the film *Vision Quest* (1984). In *Vision Quest,* high school senior Louden Swain (Matthew Modine), a wrestler, has starved and conditioned himself down two weight classes to face John Shute, the best wrestler in the state. The night of their competition brings him to a point where he entertains the idea of not competing at all. The key scene comes when he visits the night cook with whom he works at the cook's modest apartment. Swain tries to diminish the importance of the upcoming match by saying, "It's only six minutes."

That remark, and the clear sense of Louden's doubts, move the cook to tell a story about watching Pele play soccer on television. He tells of being moved to tears by Pele's performance. He sees in that athletic moment that Pele lifted "the rest of us sad ass human beings up to a better place, if only for a minute. It was goddamn glorious." Chastened, and now made aware of the importance of the competition, Louden rushes to weigh-in, finds his focus, battles Shute through blood and pain, and emerges a winner, a warrior who has recognized that sports help us to transcend ourselves, if only for a moment.

A like scene takes place in *Rudy* (1993), when, frustrated by his failure to make the final dress roster of his football career, Rudy (Sean Astin) announces that he has quit the team. With the help of the groundskeeper, an ex-Notre Dame player who had quit football and college in frustration, Rudy is brought to the recognition that he must complete the ritual he has begun, or he will live to regret it (as the groundskeeper does) for the rest of his days. Rudy makes it to the last practice, and is applauded by his fellow players, who later force the coach to not only let Rudy dress for the final game, but also to get out on the field in the last seconds of play.

In *Breaking Away,* young Dave "Enrico" Stoller is ready to give up bicycle racing entirely when his mother—who has never traveled—shows him the passport she carries in her purse to keep her own dreams alive. Now made aware that more is at stake than simple trophies, Dave goes on to lead his racing team, the "Cutters," to victory in the "Little 500."

In its own curious way, *The Air Up There* (1994) may be the film that comes closest to making explicit that the pre-game preparation component of the ritual is not simply a readying of the body and mind, but is a readying of spirit to a level where the challenger is worthy of winning. Retired professional basketball player and college scout Jimmy Dolan (Kevin Bacon) has come to Africa to recruit Sollie, a member of the Winabi tribe. Before Sollie will consider the offer, Jimmy must become a Winabi prior to playing point guard in the game that will decide the fate of Sollie's African village. His ritual of purification involves climbing a mountain. There, in a moment of self-awareness, he throws his championship ring from the mountain top; he is a man no longer bound by his past. He is then inducted into the tribe—a process that includes a ritual cutting. Now free of the selfish and self-serving self that he had brought to the village, Dolan is free to release Sollie from his promise. The game is now about more than getting a recruit to sign with the college; it is about Winabi and redemption.

In contrast, *The Longest Yard* (1974) deliberately downplays the importance of practice and training for inmate Paul Crewe (Burt Reynolds) who casually suggests that his football skills are as enduring as those of bike riding. For Crewe, the moral test and the possibility of personal redemption come only in the final quarter of play in a game where he participates honestly for a full half, then deliberately throws interceptions to get the warden the twenty-one point spread demanded. He is brought back to his internal focus partly because the warden—on a power trip of his own—reneges on the deal, and partly because Crewe recognizes—with the help of an old con—the need to play the game with integrity.

The conventional scene of recognition/reaffirmation is clearly among the most central to the sports film. While it often focuses on the necessary self doubt of the athlete, the convention is not exclusively about self-confidence. What is typically said in this scene is that the pursuit—the sport itself—is worthy of the sacrifice that the competitor must make.

In *A League of Their Own* (1992), the best player in the women's league, Dottie (Gena Davis) quits her team just as they are headed for the World Series. She has alienated her younger sister Kit because of baseball, and her husband has returned from the war. For her, it is time to go back home because, after all, "it's only a game. I don't need this." Her team manager Jimmy Dugan (Tom Hanks) tells her that she will regret her decision for the rest of her life, just as he regrets the drinking that cut five years off his distinguished career as a professional player. He tells her that "baseball is what gets inside you. It's what lights you up. You can't deny that." She protests that "it just got too hard." Dugan replies, " It's supposed to be hard. If it wasn't hard, everyone would do it. The hard's what makes it great." Although Dottie drives away, she returns in time for the last game of the World Series. She has clearly come to understand the truth of Dugan's words, his appeal to that which "lights you up" to the "hard" that makes it great.

Scenes of recognition and awareness are the scenes in sports films where a social group has a chance to participate in the ritual of the sport. The athlete, who must, in the final moment, stand alone (even in the most integrated team sports), must be brought to recognize that what he or she does extends beyond the boundaries of personal need. Sport, in these films, has meaning that goes beyond simple organized play or formalized competition, to become a ritual fraught with meaning and symbolic potency. The competitors realize in the moment of recognition/reaffirmation, the game or match or race is not simply about itself. It is a ritual about human potential, a sacrament of the body and mind in which the competitor and the spectators have a moment in which they can transcend their own limits. Sports provide an arena for the reaffirmation of some of our most important social values.

At the crudest level, these films suggest that all those things that the football coach said about the value of the game are true. At another level, the films seem to suggest that the coach hardly grasped a portion of the importance of the game, the match, or the race. In many of the films discussed here—and in dozens of other sport-centered films—the game, the match, or the race are rituals of celebration of an illusive but real human transcendence. In its best moments, sports are shown to transport us—both participants and viewers—outside ourselves. For a moment, the athlete partakes of the divine. As runner Eric Liddell (Ian Charleson) says in *Chariots of Fire* (1981): "I believe God made me for a purpose, and when I run I can feel his pleasure." Liddell, a pastor by profession, expresses and embodies the true spirit of the Olympic games in which he runs in the film. As the ancient Greeks would have us remember, there is a powerful and sacred relationship between the body and the soul of the athlete.

Perhaps the most familiar of the conventions of the sports film is the final phase, the mobbing scene. This scene—which is commonplace at both real and movie sporting events—has dimensions that clearly go beyond the simple acknowledgment of victory. The mobbing scene, that moment when both spectators and winners merge in celebration of the event itself, is typically an orgy of touching and physical contact both for participants and spectators. Besides exalting leaps, cheers, and celebratory arms thrown skyward, mobbing scenes allow—indeed seem to demand—hugging and kissing not only between teammates and/or their significant others, but among total strangers as well. The mobbing scene in sports films has all the characteristics of a true ritual occasion, where community is celebrated unabashedly.

Indeed, the convention is so well established that in films like *Major League* (1989) and *A League of Their Own,* the convention is referentially used. In *Major League,* Roger Dorn (Corbin Bernsen) first punches his teammate Wild Thing (Charlie Sheen) for sleeping with his wife, then embraces him. In a shot in a Cleveland bar where the patrons are celebrating the pennant victory, a working-class guy in a gimme cap self-consciously pauses and then embraces a full dressed punker. In *A League of Their Own,* a male patron seated next to the league manager is clearly non-plussed at being embraced by another male.

In *Hoosiers* (1986), the team and coach are mobbed at the conclusion of the state championships, and even the most doubting of the town fathers joins in a celebration of hugging, as does the hospitalized "Shooter" (Dennis Hopper), who rushes to embrace the lone nurse on his floor. In *The Longest Yard,* the prisoner spectators swirl in physical celebration; in *Breaking Away* a crowd descends on the "Cutter" team in their victory. All of the *Rocky* films have ring and ringside mobbing. Rudy is mobbed and carried from the stadium on his teammates' shoulders. Louden Swain is engulfed in celebrants as is Hobbes (Robert Redford) in *The Natural* (1984), and virtually every victor in a sports film.

Mobbing, with its explosion of touching and physical contact, seems like more than simple elation or appreciation. Rather, mobbing seems a true celebration of the physical exploits of the athlete with another kind of physicality. It seems as if cheering and applause are not enough; the event has broken the barriers of physical and emotional constraint, and must be acknowledged physically within the community of participants and spectators. This need is nowhere more evident than the celebration scene in *The Air Up There,* where the fattest member of the team has his belly rubbed and kissed, and even the nun cannot restrain herself from kissing Jimmy Dolan squarely on the mouth.

Between the convention of mobbing and the pattern of scenes of recognition/awareness, sports films seem—as a group—to suggest that sports are, after all, more than recreation, more than means to personal ends, and more than personal testing grounds. In film after film, sports are presented as true rituals whose true purpose is the redemption of those who can truly enter its spirit.

The Natural, with its clear pattern of other worldliness and magic, is like *Field of Dreams* (1989), a film that insists on the transcendence of baseball. In both films, baseball is a path toward the spiritual, a rite played out for the benefit not only of the players, but of the fans as well—particularly the children. In *Field of Dreams,* Mann (James Earl Jones) tells Kinsella (Kevin Costner) that his child is right, that masses of people will come to sit on his bleachers and watch a magical diamond. Mann says they will come not quite knowing why, but driven by a deep nostalgia for a more innocent time, for a history that is fraught with meaning. For Kinsella, the field itself is a vehicle toward redemption; he can, at last, make peace with his father as they toss a ball between them.

That *The Natural* begins and ends with that same ritual of catch between father and son helps make it clear that tossing the ball back and forth is more than simple play or exercise; it is, in fact, a communion. Sport simplified to its most basic elements, a ball and two players without even a hint of competition, is a rite of bonding, a communion between the generations, an acknowledgment of tradition and of the simple but rich pleasures that baseball affords.

The Natural and *Field of Dreams* make it clear that sports and redemption are fused. In less mystical ways, films like *The Air Up There, The Longest Yard, Breaking Away,* and *Major League* also suggest that sports are not about play in the trivial sense, nor simply about competition or winning; sports in these films are about reconciliation and redemption. The athlete or the team achieves some purpose beyond whatever the obvious rewards of winning might be. Crewe, in *The Longest Yard,* redeems his personal integrity, gives heart to the prison population, and probably destroys the career of the abusive warden. In *A League of Their Own,* Jimmy Dugan finds a place for himself away from the bottle; Kit emerges from the shadow of her more talented sister, and the sisters eventually become close. In *Major League,* the team's victory not only saves the franchise for Cleveland, it revitalizes the city, and seems to bring Jake Taylor's (Tom Berringer) wife back to him. In *All the Right Moves* (1983), the coach comes to realize the error of his ways, and offers Stefan Djorjevic (Tom Cruise) a full scholarship, a way out of the dying mill town. In *Rudy,* Rudy's moment of triumph extends to his family, particularly his cynical brother, and we are told in a title that all of his younger siblings completed college. *Rocky,* of course, was an archetypal film of redemption; the bone-breaking small time hood transformed himself into a contender and a family man.

In *Breaking Away,* father and son find common ground, Mike (Dennis Quaid) is reconciled with his brother the cop, and the pride of the "Cutters" is restored. In *Hoosiers,* the least athletic player makes the two free throws that win the championship, and is carried in a victory round; coach Norman Dale (Gene Hackman), who had been banished for life by the NCAA has become a coach again; Shooter, the alcoholic assistant coach, is on his way to recovery, and Myra Flechner (Barbara Hersey), the skeptical English teacher, has come to recognize that basketball is worth celebrating.

The list of redemptive sports moments in Hollywood films seems nearly endless, but we must remember that the event itself in each film is the focal point; even in *The Air Up There,* where the stakes of the game are an entire village, the real meaning of the victory is personal redemption. Jimmy Dolan becomes a man of real integrity at the same time that the chief of the village is reconciled with his wayward son and the village itself is revitalized.

This body of Hollywood sports movies suggests Victor Turner's definition of ritual as "prescribed formal behavior of occasions not given over to technological routine, having reference to beliefs in invisible being or powers regarded as first and final causes of all effects" (14). Sports films themselves have become the dominant American film genre, one which has become an American ritual.[4] As film scholar Howard Good points out, films about baseball "are older than the World Series," and, although the baseball movie has always seemed a financial risk to Hollywood producers, there are a substantial number of movies in which baseball serves in some capacity (134). "Whatever else they are," Good writes about baseball movies, "they are complex, allusive, multi-layered works in which magic and religion, physical objects, and psychological states, the myths of Hollywood and Cooperstown, converge" (135).

Good also suggests that the surge of Hollywood baseball films in the 1980s and '90s is a "means of conveying ideological values, particularly the conservative values of America's rural past" (135). The steady stream of baseball movies during this time: *The Natural, Bull Durham* (1988), *Field of Dreams, A League of Their Own,* to name only a few, would seem to bear this out. Good suggests that baseball movies "aren't really about baseball," but are "mythical versions of our own life stories, our own trying passages through time and change" (147).[5]

Through the second half of the twentieth century, the most sacred, most traditional, most serious of rituals have gradually been used against themselves, and have become the symbols and signals for any number of moments of disaster or disappointment in movies. The small moments of genuine illumination in most Hollywood productions come in quiet, understated ways. Films in which the rituals of the sport become the means to our understanding of something else—whether it be a search for Kinsella's father in *Field of Dreams* or the female league's quest for respect in *A League of Their Own*—fill an important void for American moviegoers. Only the sports film allows us both the integrity of a ritual occasion and the luminosity of the moment.

"We need heroes," writes Good in the concluding paragraph in his essay on baseball films. He continues:

Living in the dying moments of the twentieth century, surrounded by ghosts and abandoned gods, we face, individually and collectively, vexing questions about who we are and where we are headed. Baseball films offer an answer of sorts. (147)

The need for and popularity of sports films represents our best clue to the changing rituals in American culture and Hollywood films. There are countless sports films which remind us that the symbols of celebration we might have seen imbedded in sacred or traditional rituals in earlier decades now appear in movies about athletic competitions. Children's rituals, once used to indicate maturity or achievement, as in *A Tree Grows in Brooklyn* and *Our Very Own,* have become either absent from Hollywood films, as in *The Graduate,* or are ritual occasions in parody, as in *Reality Bites.* We see, instead, children and teenagers who begin to respect the values of their culture, and who seem to gain self-respect, in movies where these children are aspiring athletes: *The Bad News Bears* (1976), *The Karate Kid* films of the 1980s, *Breaking Away, Vision Quest, Hoosiers,* and *Higher Learning* (1994). In these films, and in others like them, we watch young athletes learning about honesty, vigilance, and loyalty as they strive with their bodies to achieve excellence within their souls.

Instead of luminous graduation scenes, we watch scenes of profound joy as young athletes beat the odds and win athletic competitions. Dave (Dennis Christopher) and his team of "cutters" win the Little Indianapolis 500-bicycle race, and bask in the glow of their families' and friends' enthusiastic celebration of their victory in *Breaking Away.* Loudon Swain (Matthew Modine), struggling high school wrestler, finally moves from immaturity to maturity when he wins the big match in *Vision Quest.* Although we know that he is a graduating senior who wants to study medicine, his excellence comes on the wrestling mat, and our last shot of him is as he is carried out of the gym by his joyous teammates.

The ritual "big games" and "big wins" of adult sports professionals have become the moments of illumination as well, long ago displacing scenes of traditional ritual occasions to show us love, honor, or faith. The moment of truth for Roy Hobbs (Robert Redford) in *The Natural* comes on the baseball diamond, where he sees his long-abandoned true love Iris (Glenn Close), luminously lit up for him in the stands. When Roy hits his final dramatic home run into the lights of the stadium, he does so with the knowledge that his new-found family of Iris and her (his?) son are in the stands, and his love for them steadies and fortifies him.

The moments when we celebrate in Hollywood films are closely related to the world of sports, and there are countless scenes where we do celebrate. *Rocky* (1976) ends not with a wedding, but with a sweaty ring-side admonition of love between Rocky Balboa (Sylvester Stallone) and his girlfriend Adrienne (Talia Shire). In *Field of Dreams,* although we know that Ray's (Kevin Costner's) obsession with his farmland baseball field is related to his grief at the loss of his father, we never see anything in the film to suggest mourning or funerals. What we see, instead, is the joy of the sport and the celebration of life.

In sport film after sport film, the play becomes the means to transcendence; the trophy, prestige, scholarship, (or whatever material ends) are at most emblems of a transcendent moment. At their most profound moments, American sports movies suggest that sports are a ritual, one in which the spectacle of competition and athletic prowess lift "the rest of us sad ass human beings up to a better place, if only for a moment."

Since the years of World War II, Hollywood films have increasingly portrayed traditional ritual occasions as diminished, transparent rites, and sports as rituals of dignity and solemnity. Audiences know the difference, for both are established traditions in Hollywood film. An American audience in the 1990s will understand the ritual of hard-won victory in a sports film with the same degree of familiarity as it does when it recognizes a traditional scene of a ritual occasion in a movie. Both are essential elements in a formula of symbols provided by Hollywood. Luminous sports films and those smaller luminous moments of parent/child bedtimes, dancing, swimming, are ritualized and encoded into movies in ways that suggest they are legitimate rituals themselves.

Scenes of ritual occasions represent the underside of ritualized moments of transcendence. An American audience in the mid-1990s knows that a wedding celebration will turn into a chaotic mess, or that a funeral will be whimsical or entertaining, and that these scenes will not necessarily be scenes into which characters or audiences will invest many profound feelings. Ritual scenes tell us something other than about our feelings. Instead, the scenes of rituals in Hollywood films tell us much about the American culture of which Hollywood is part.

The various ritual occasions we have reviewed, and the examples of the most powerful, popular, or significant scenes of rituals reveal a great deal about the Hollywood environment out of which these scenes have been generated. That most scenes of ritual occasions, until very recently, have reflected only a portion of the ethnic, racial, or religious segments of the American population tells us something we probably already knew: Hollywood's stories have always represented a dominant culture, portraying its rites and rituals in ways which, as we have seen, poked and prodded at these rituals until they have come to mean the opposite of what we might expect on screen.

We see few birthday parties for any children (or adults) other than white children; wedding celebrations for couples other than privileged white ones are few, and the weddings of Hispanic, Asian, or African American couples are either implied or are scenes of disaster or comic relief. Funerals are often scenes where we only see the superficial symbols of grief, and funerals for people of color show them to be martyrs and victims, caught in webs of racial or economic distress.

Scenes of ritual occasions in films since 1945 have become increasingly problematic, reflecting not the celebrations and triumphs of American culture in stories on film, but its vulnerabilities and hypocrisies. Ritual scenes show us not so much the importance of how we mark rites of passage in our lives, but how we neglect or disrespect these rites. Our ritual occasions, Hollywood films tell us, are not the point. The point, these ritual scenes suggest, has more to do with the luminous moments of movies—the fleeting moments of genuine pleasure or pain which "light us up"—than it does with the traditional ritual occasions of our culture.

Scenes of rituals and moments of luminosity are both part of the fabric of Hollywood art. They provide the dark and the light, the static moment and the moving picture, the continuity and the shock of the new that characterize Hollywood film. When we watch a scene of a ritual occasion in a mainstream American production, we are always watching something else, and we are rarely allowed the pleasure of celebration. These scenes, far from giving us safe reproductions of traditions and mores, reflect an edgy, uncompromising approach to ritual occasions which project the American culture that Hollywood sees: our public, bright rituals look beautiful, but they are a dramatic illusion. Ritual occasions neither represent nor reflect our happiness or triumph or sorrow, but our fears and our unfulfilled needs.

The movies, a highly formal, ritualized medium, seem to fill any number of needs for American society. Moviegoing and the movies represent ritual occasions in which the fusion of commerce, technology, and storytelling suggests to the transfixed audience the ideals of a "divine, human, animal and vegetative cosmos of mores, moralities, and mutual relationships" (17). We make our way to the holy site, pay our admission, buy food to sustain us, surrender our tickets, enter the semi-darkened room to sit and wait in ordered rows the coming of the vast illusion, a tale told with light, as insubstantial as a dream, shared with strangers who are part of the experience. Still later, with friends or family, we will discuss that experience in terms that have less to do with life than with illusion. Our ritual occasions may have changed, but we still need them. Moviegoing comes close to transcending the need for ritual celebrations of our culture.

Where we feel most comfortable, where we see most clearly, is in the dark, alone. Watching movies, in the dark and alone, has indeed become a ritual that celebrates itself over and over in American film. Although European and Asian films have long celebrated film in film, most poignantly in, for instance, the Italian production of *Cinema Paradiso* (1989), the American film community has been reluctant or uncomfortable when celebrating unabashedly the beauty and power of storytelling on film.

There are, however, some American films which do allow us the chance to see the power of movies in the movies; our best example of this sacred significance of film comes in an American film which fails on many levels, yet shows clearly Hollywood's ability to celebrate its art. *Once Around* (1990) is a movie where scenes of ritual occasions—from weddings, to baptisms, to religious holidays, to funerals—almost suffocate any semblance of narrative, yet this film includes a remarkable example of the relationship of ritual scenes to luminous moments in American film.

Renata (Holly Hunter) is a young woman whose boyfriend has dumped her on the night of her sister's wedding. Distraught, Renata travels to the Caribbean to train for a new job, only to fall in love with her trainer, salesman and extrovert Sam Sharp (Richard Dreyfess). After Renata and Sam marry, (theirs is the second wedding we attend in the film), we begin to understand how tentatively Sam is accepted into Renata's close knit family. We watch a montage of scenes of strained family dinners and holiday occasions at Renata's parents' home, and this montage helps us to understand two important time-passage developments in the film narrative: Renata's family cannot seem to warm to Sam, and Renata is pregnant.

In a family dinner scene where Renata looks to be about nine months' pregnant, Sam irritates the family one time too many, and Renata's mother (Gena Rowlands) asks Renata to banish Sam from further family gatherings. The couple leaves, and we next see Renata lying on a couch in her darkened living room, bare, ripe belly shining in the light of a television screen. As she lies there talking to Sam, we notice that what she is watching is a video of an old home movie.

On her pregnant belly radiates the image of a toddler on the beach, of a mother hugging a baby. The two of them watch the video's reflection silently. In a movie full of silly, vacuous scenes of ritual occasions, this is the most significant and pure scene of love and celebration that we see. The luminous moments of Hollywood films appear in the dark, in silence, on film, and often in places and in movies where we least expect to find them.[6]

From the epic grandeur and violence of rituals in *The Godfather*, to this small moment in the small movie *Once Around*, we understand that the power of a Hollywood film lies in its ability to provide us with terrifying and beautiful reproductions of traditional ritual occasions. Yet in its reflections of the trivial moments of life, the movies can catch the small luminous moments which make us a human community as well. A moving picture camera, in the darkness of our everyday lives and in our dreams, allows our changing rituals to become sacred or profane. Hollywood films, before and since 1945, offer us this gift in the dark and light of a screen: a spectrum of light both refracted and reflected. If we look one way, we see the pageantry and dangers of our rituals and traditions. If we look the other way, we see ourselves, in the movies, celebrating our humanity.

AFTERWORD

Among the thousands of American films that include scenes of ritual occasions, there are a few remarkable scenes in which the ritual occasions and luminous transcendence are fused. When Tevya's oldest daughter marries in *Fiddler on the Roof* (1971), her wedding, complete with song, candlelight, and tears, becomes a ceremony where we are part of a community of people who truly love each other. In *Crimes of the Heart*, Lenny (Diane Keaton) is surprised with a birthday celebration by her two sisters Babe (Sissy Spacek) and Meg (Jessica Lange) in the final scene of the film. The three sisters sing, dance, and cry their way through their private party, and we understand how much they love each other by the glow of all three of their faces as they sing.

When Karen Blixen (Meryl Streep) reads A. E. Housman's poem, "To an Athlete Dying Young," at the funeral of her lover Denys Finch-Hatton (Robert Redford) in *Out of Africa* (1985), her voice cracks as she concludes. "You were never ours," she says quietly, "you were never mine." As the other mourners look on, Blixen picks up a handful of dirt, and leans over, ready to throw it into the grave. She hesitates for a moment, clasps the dirt to her bosom, and turns away. We are the only ones present at this burial who understand enough about the depth of the relationship she had with Finch-Hatton to grieve with her as she walks out into the Nairobi landscape alone.

In *Four Weddings and a Funeral* (1993) Matthew (John Hannah) speaks at the funeral of his companion Gareth (Simon Callow). When he reminds his listeners of how eccentric Gareth was, we see close-ups of the faces of the mourners; some are smiling, some are crying, some are nodding in agreement with Matthew. We also watch Gareth's mother's face while Matthew speaks, and for several seconds, we can feel the anguish of this mother who has lost a child.

Matthew concludes his eulogy by reading a poem by W. H. Auden. "Stop all the clocks, cut off the telephone," he reads, and indeed, all action stops for a second. As he continues to read, we watch the mourners leaving the church. As Gareth's casket is placed in the waiting hearse, we hear Matthew's final line "Pour away the ocean and sweep up the woods/For nothing now can ever come to any good."

In a film full of stylish, funny weddings which swirl around us in quick succession, this lone and solemn funeral stands out as the most sacred ritual occasion presented to us. The funeral sequence is distinguished not just by the solemnity of the occasion, but by the setting, which is also quite different from those of the three weddings. The church is small and unassuming, and as Gareth's mourners stand outside, we notice that, unlike the stylish neighborhoods of the weddings in the film, we are in an industrialized suburb of London for this truly sorrowful funeral.

Like the funeral in *Out of Africa,* the funeral in *Four Weddings and a Funeral* allows us to be mourners as well as observers. In both films, the audience has been privy to scenes of private moments between the two sets of couples. We understand, more than any of the other mourners at the funerals, the depth of sorrow created by the loss of Denys and Gareth. Karen Blixen's and Matthew's losses become our losses, too; the loneliness of mourning becomes a shared ritual between those characters on the screen and the audience.

These truly genuine moments shared by characters and audiences are rare and fleeting, and they may suggest that ritual occasions are most effective when they are left to an audience's imagination. Indeed, in some of the American movies where we might expect to see representations of ritual occasions which seem to have significance to the plots or character development, these occasions are merely mentioned or implied. Benjamin's missing graduation scene in *The Graduate* is only one of several implied scenes of ritual occasions in Hollywood productions.

In *The War of the Roses,* a film in which we follow in a series of flashbacks the courtship, marriage, divorce, and destruction of Oliver and Barbara Rose (Michael Douglas and Kathleen Turner), we are denied the memory of their wedding. After living through a decade of the on-again-off-again relationship of Harry and Sally (Billy Crystal and Meg Ryan) in *When Harry Met Sally* (1989), we understand that they are married in the last scene because they tell us so, but we were not invited to their wedding in the film. Likewise in *Gone with the Wind,* the only way we know that Scarlet finally marries Rhett is that we see them on their honeymoon. Finally, the *Godfather* epic, which can be characterized as a monumental tribute to ritual occasions on film, does not include a wedding ceremony for Michael and Kay, nor a funeral for Michael. This is not accidental; that we watch Michael's courtship and marriage—and wedding night—to his first wife in Sicily, and that we never see any suggestion of a wedding scene between him and Kay, suggests to us that Michael's first marriage had a sanctity and significance that his second marriage does not. We see many funerals in the *Godfather* films, most notably those of Michael's parents, yet Michael, himself a Don in Vito Corleone's empire, gets no final elaborate ritual occasion in the film by which we can mark his life.

Funerals are especially notable in films by their absence, perhaps because funerals suggest the loneliness of grief in ways that films can rarely capture. We watch death scenes often: Emma (Debra Winger) in *Terms of Endearment;* Jenny (Ali McGraw) in *Love Story;* Maverick (Anthony Edwards) in *Top Gun.* Yet we do not watch their loved ones bury them or grieve together during their funerals in these movies. Occasionally the suggestion of a funeral becomes a most significant point of the film, as in *Ordinary People.*

Calvin (Donald Sutherland) and Beth (Mary Tyler Moore) have lost their older son Buck in a drowning accident which their younger son Conrad (Timothy Hutton) survived. Two years have passed when we meet the family, and Conrad is now trying to recover from a suicide attempt and subsequent hospitalization. We watch as all of the characters attempt to come to terms with their loss and with their lives in the present. They live and talk carefully and with control; we rarely hear them mention Buck or his death.

During one scene, Calvin has gone to see Conrad's psychiatrist (Judd Hirsch) to talk about Conrad's problems. During the course of their conversation, Calvin realizes that he has really come to talk about his own problems. Although we do not hear any further dialogue between the two men, we do know what they discussed, because in the next scene, Calvin, disoriented and disheveled, returns home and pleads with Beth: "Can we talk about Buck's funeral?" She reluctantly agrees, and he recalls for her that on the day of their son's funeral, she was upset about his choice of shoes and socks to wear. "What difference did it make what I wore to Buck's funeral?" he asks her. "I was crazy that day. We were going to our son's funeral. And you were worried about what I wore on my feet."

This encounter between Calvin and Beth becomes a major turning point for them and for us in *Ordinary People*. Calvin has begun the painful process of grieving for Buck by talking about his feelings with his wife (whose resistance to the discussion will continue to fester throughout the remainder of the film). For us, the suggestion of the funeral and its power and pain has contributed to our understanding of their relationship and their behavior in ways that we would never have had, had we actually watched the funeral ritual itself. It is the memory of the day that becomes important to Calvin and through his dialogue, he creates a memory that allows us to share the unimaginable anguish of two parents who were "crazy" that day.

That we notice when ritual occasions are missing, attests to the power of ritual occasions on film. Whether they are implied or suggested, whether they recreate cultural rituals in profane or sacred ways, all ritual occasions in American movies represent one of our most profound gauges to how we project and present our stories in the movies. Nowhere else but in the movies can we find the complexities of our lives, dreams and fears better recreated for us, and in no better way can we begin to understand the richness of American culture and American film than by studying the spectrum of our ritual occasions offered to us in the movies.

NOTES

Chapter 1

1. There are no other full-length studies of ritual occasions in Hollywood films, although many sources have been useful. We will note those sources which deal with specific films, or with specific rituals in film, as we continue our discussion. We have included a complete and comprehensive list of useful sources and works cited at the end of the book, as well as a complete filmography.

2. There are many good discussions of *The Godfather* films. We have been helped by the following general discussions of the films: Thomson's chapter, "The Discreet Charm of the Godfather," in *Overexposures;* Johnson; Nichols; Denby, *America in the Dark;* and Shadoian, *Dreams and Dead Ends*. For more on rituals in the *Godfather* films, see Chapter 3 of this study.

3. For an excellent discussion of the relationships of men and women in *The Godfather* films, see Haskell, *From Reverence to Rape*.

4. We have relied on several scholarly essays and books which deal with the sociology and anthropology of rituals and festivals. Most useful have been the works by Victor Turner, especially *The Ritual Process: Structure and Anti-Structure* and *Dramas, Fields, and Metaphors*. All of these anthropological or sociological works can be found in our "Works Cited" section.

Chapter 2

1. For other readings on rites of passage, see Turner, *Dramas, Fields, and Metaphors;* Abrahams, and Grimes.

2. For another discussion *of A Tree Grows in Brooklyn*, see Loukides, "The Celebration of Family Plot."

3. Perhaps the saddest of all juvenile birthday parties comes in the 1937 production of *Stella Dallas*. For excellent discussions of this film, and of "women's films" of the 1930s, '40s, and '50s, see espe-

cially Byars, Doane, Kaplan, Williams, "Something Else Besides a Mother," and Doane, Mellencamp, and Williams, eds., *Re-Visions*.

4. For general discussions on the significance of *The Graduate*, see Alpert, Cagin and Dray, Kolker, and Ray.

5. There are many other examples of films in which children are put in difficult, sometimes harrowing adult-sized situations. In the spirit of Truffaut's *The Four Hundred Blows* (1959), Hollywood has produced many films where children find themselves in harm's way. Among the most notable are *The Night of the Hunter* (1955), *The Diary of Anne Frank* (1959), *To Kill a Mockingbird* (1962), *The Exorcist* (1973), *Witness* (1985), *Empire of the Sun* (1987), *Au Revoir, Les Enfants* (1987), *Europa, Europa* (1990), *Radio Flyer* (1992), *This Boy's Life* (1993), and *The Client* (1994).

6. In addition to the many bad juvenile birthday parties, there are innumerable adult birthday parties which are disappointments or nightmares. In fact, there are few birthday parties in any Hollywood productions that turn out to be celebratory affairs. Perhaps Hollywood took its cue from F. Scott Fitzgerald's narrator Nick in *The Great Gatsby*, who forgets his own thirtieth birthday. Bad or sad birthday party scenes show up in *The Courtship of Eddie's Father* (1963), *The Great Gatsby* (1974), *Tootsie* (1982), *Terms of Endearment* (1983), *The Music Box* (1989), *Driving Miss Daisy* (1989), *Eating* (1991), *City Slickers* (1991), *Boys on the Side* (1995), and *Waiting to Exhale* (1995).

7. Aaron's award for scholarship suggests another type of ritual ceremony popular in Hollywood productions, one that shows up in both juvenile and adult narratives: the award ceremony. Again, when awards ceremonies show up as concluding scenes, as in *Star Wars* (1977) or the 1954 production of *A Star Is Born*, they most often contribute to a sense of closure for both characters and audience. However, when imbedded in films, scenes of award ceremonies signal complications and problems, as in *The Best Years of Our Lives* (1946), *The Blue Max* (1966), *Cross of Iron* (1977), and *Catch 22* (1970). In *Catch 22*, each of the individual crew members of Yossarian's bomber is awarded a medal for dumping their bomb load into the sea and killing fish. The alternative is to court marshal them for disobeying an order to bomb a defenseless and strategically unimportant town. Yossarian attends the award ceremony start naked; both the medal and the ceremony are utter shams.

Award ceremonies often create a sense of cynicism and defeat—as when Eve wins an award at the beginning of *All About Eve* (1950), or when the less talented, less honest beauty contestant wins the county beauty pageant in *Smile* (1975). The cynically political citation given to Clint Eastwood in *The Enforcer* (1976) helps illuminate the pervasive nature of the loss of public ideals. *L.A. Confidential* (1997), a film that pays homage to many classic film devices, includes two awards scenes where we understand the bogus nature of the awards being given to police officers.

Awards, as secular acknowledgments of secular accomplishments, rarely suggest a sense of transcendence or luminescence. In a society where there are awards for salesmen of the month, and students with the best attendance records, movie awards are often no more than a passing acknowledgment of minor distinctions, and perhaps as often are used as commentaries on the shallowness or corruption of the secular worlds that they celebrate.

Chapter 3

1. There are several discussions of particular wedding scenes discussed in this essay, including Brode's essay on *Father of the Bride*. There are also helpful essays on related topics: romantic comedy in Harvey, and the comedy of remarriage in Cavell, and several essays in *Multiple Voices in Feminist Film Criticism* mention various Hollywood treatments of marriage. For other related discussions, see Haskell and Maio.

This chapter is a revision of an earlier essay, "The Pleasure of Our Company: Hollywood Throws a Wedding Bash," by Parley Ann Boswell, in *Beyond the Stars* Volume II, ed. Paul Loukides and Linda K. Fuller (Bowling Green, OH: Bowling Green State University Popular Press, 1991).

2. The best discussions of the interrupted (or peculiar) weddings of the 1930s and '40s are in Cavell and Harvey. There are many good discussions of *The Graduate*, among them Alpert, "The Graduate Makes Out," and Cagin and Dray, who point out very aptly the problems we might have with Benjamin's and Elaine's final scene: "They don't know where they are going and neither do we, and we have been given no reason to believe they will manage adulthood any differently than their parents" (32).

3. There are significant discussions of ethnicity in both *Goodbye Columbus* and *The Heartbreak Kid* in Erens, *The Jew in American Cinema*. Erens points out that the wedding reception scene in *Goodbye Columbus* "drew heavy cricism for its poor taste and shades of anti-Semitism," but she makes a solid case for the value of the scene: "The chaos and commotion, the abundance of food, the noise, all of these are accurate and neither innately positive or negative . . ." (275).

4. For more on the maltreatment of women in *The Godfather* films, see especially Yates, and Haskell, who characterizes *The Godfather*—I think accurately—as a "womanless melodrama" (23).

5. Rubin Wood describes the "spilt wine" scene as one of the "great poetic moments where the tension crystalizes" because the audience is allowed to "put things together": "the moment anticipates the blood of Vietnam and Steven's loss of his legs," and the moment also allows us to see Steven's "split allegiance" between Angela and his male friends (283).

6. Wood cites this scene as a "second great poetic moment" in the film; he compares the Green Beret in the bar to the Ancient Mariner: ". . . though he has returned to America [he] is no longer 'of' it" (283).

7. There are many good essays on *The Deer Hunter*. Wood's is particularly helpful because he includes a lengthy discussion of each sequence of scenes in the film. Other helpful studies include Boyd and Wilson. Two helpful general discussions of Vietnam war movies are Adair, and Auster and Quart.

8. Other Hollywood productions where weddings serve to further plot lines or help us discover characters are many; an incomplete list would include: *Broadcast News* (1987), *Cousins* (1989), the 1975 French production of *Cousin, Cousine*, *Coming to America* (1988), *Crimes and Misdemeanors* (1989), *Giant* (1956), *Gone with the Wind* (1939), *High Noon* (1952), *Light in the Piazza* (1962), *Out of Africa* (1985), *Prelude to a Kiss* (1992), *Rocky II* (1979), *Steel Magnolias* (1989), *The Stranger* (1946), *True Love* (1990), *Turner and Hootch* (1989), *Twice in a Lifetime* (1985), *Valmont* (1989), and *When Harry Met Sally* (1989). Funny weddings—weddings where one or more of the participants make mistakes or do something unexpected—also show up in many films, including *Beaches* (1988), *Best Friends*

(1982), *Cocoon* (1985), and *Four Weddings and a Funeral* (1994). The lists are truly endless; weddings are one of Hollywood's most popular and versatile plot devices.

9. There are some truly nightmarish weddings scenes in American movies. Among them is, ironically enough, a scene in a classic Hollywood musical, *Oklahoma!* (1955). A wedding in *Four Friends* (1981), seems to be one of the worst wedding days in American film history: the bride's father apparently snaps and pulls out a gun during the reception. He shoots his daughter to death, and maims her groom before turning the gun on himself, all in view of the wedding guests.

10. The histories and importance of ethnic actors, films, directors, and writers in the Hollywood story are finally being treated by scholars, and there are some very fine studies, among them the works by Bogle, Cripps, Freydberg, hooks, Gibson-Hudson, and especially Friedman, *Unspeakable Images; Ethnicity and the American Cinema.* For a very fine study of Asians and interraciality in Hollywood films, see Marchetti, *Romance and the "Yellow Peril."*

11. There is a fine discussion of *Sayonara* in Marchetti's chapter, "Tragic and Transcendent Love: *Sayonara* and *The Crimson Kimono*" in *Romance and the "Yellow Peril."*

12. In his chapter on Altman, Kolker points out that it "is difficult not to be angry with [*A Wedding*] . . . Its cleverness always threatens to become smugness, a smugness that is always at the expense of its characters, and finally at ours" (328). Other discussions of *A Wedding* are in Thomson, and in McGilligan's biography of Altman.

Chapter 4

1. By 1909, D. W. Griffith had directed over one hundred one-reel films, and had filmed several funeral scenes, including one in *A Corner of Wheat* and in *Ramona* (1911). For discussions of Griffith's work, see Cook, *A History of Narrative Film,* chapter three, and Griffith's autobiography, *The Man Who Invented Hollywood.* Also see Martin Williams, *Griffith: First Artist of the Movies.*

2. There are many good works on American Westerns. Especially helpful is John Nachbar, *Focus on the Western.* Also useful to our study is Marsden's essay "Western Films: America's Secularized Religion."

Also see the chapter "The Discrepancy between Intent and Effect: *Film Noir,* Youth Rebellion Pictures, Musicals, and Westerns" in Ray, *A Certain Tendency of the Hollywood Cinema.*

3. There are many good works on American war movies. The most useful to our study of funerals in the movies have been Ray's chapter "Classic Hollywood's Holding Pattern: The Combat Films of World War II," in *A Certain Tendency of the Hollywood Cinema;* Suid, *Guts and Glory;* and Jacobs, "World War II and the American Film."

4. From Shakespeare's tragedies and histories (*Hamlet, Henry IV*), to the novels of Jane Austen and George Eliot (*Sense and Sensibility, The Mill on the Floss*), and into the twentieth-century novels of E. M. Forster, William Faulkner, and Toni Morrison, much of literature shares this characteristic: action begins when someone dies.

We have found the works by Parish and Pitts, *The Great Detective Pictures,* and by Selby, *Dark City,* most useful to this study.

5. In an odd sub-category of the military funeral—the Viking funeral—the funeral is both a rite and a spectacle. In *The Vikings* (1958), *The Long Ships* (1964), *Excalibur* (1981), and most recently in *First Knight* (1997), the audience is invited to recognize that this special sort of funeral is just recognition of the unique status of the deceased. In this spectacular rite, the values of the hero and of the group that launches him to sea are reaffirmed.

In contrast, the launching into space of the body of a fallen comrade in *Starship Troopers* (1997) seems as ordinary as a ground burial in a contemporary film, and no more redemptive. Ironically, the comic "Viking funeral" in *S.O.B.* (1981), has a greater sense of reaffirmation. The drunken friends who steal the corpse from the funeral parlor know that the planned funeral will be an empty Hollywood sham. Instead, they take their comrade to shore, put him in a row boat, douse him with gasoline, and let him drift away as the fire rises. Acting out of alcoholically heightened love and friendship, they enact a ritual stolen from Hollywood costume dramas to say their last farewells. As in the costume films, the values of the decedent and of the group which launches him to sea are reaffirmed.

6. For excellent discussions on *Imitation of Life,* see Byars, chapter five of *All That Hollywood Allows;* Hueng, Marina, "What's the Matter with Sara Jane?"; Winokur, "Black Is White/White Is Black";

Stubbs and Freydberg, "Black Women in American Films"; and Bogle, *Toms, Coons, Mulattoes, Mammies, and Bucks.*

Chapter Five

1. For a fine essay on *American Graffiti,* see Sodowsky, Sodowsky, and Witte, "The Epic World of *American Graffiti.*"

2. There are some wonderful moments of illumination in Hollywood film, and, like all good cinema, they defy categorization in many ways. We have chosen these three ways—bedtime scenes, dancing scenes, and bath/rain/swimming scenes not arbitrarily, but with some hesitation, because scenes where we become engaged in moments of clarity or unselfconscious behavior show up everywhere. Our categories are intended to be useful only as a point of departure for our scholarship. To be honest, these moments delight us precisely because they do not respond readily to scholarship at all.

3. Sports in the movies, especially baseball movies, have been the subject of many good essays. Particularly useful to our study have been the following: Bergan, *Sports in the Movies;* Good, "Extra Innings"; Ardolino, "Ceremonies of Innocence"; and Sayre, "Winning the Weepstakes." On football in the movies, see Noverr.

4. Besides Good's and Wiggins' essays, there are other good works that discuss the relationship among sports, ritual, violence, and film. Additional useful sources to this study have been MacAloon, who contemplates the ritual of the American Super Bowl; Joseph Campbell's work on "the hero" in *The Hero With a Thousand Faces,* and most especially Richard Slotkin's very fine essay, "Prologue to a Study of Myth and Genre in American Movies," which has been useful not just because of his discussion of sports movies, but because he deals with the significance of symbols and mythologies of several American movie genres, discussing, for instance, the relationship among combat films, Westerns, and sports films.

5. Good and Ardolino both mention another 1980s film, *Eight Men Out,* as being a film which does not reflect the sentimentality of other 1980s baseball films. This film "offers the grimmest portrayal of sloppy baseball as moral corruption," writes Good. "Fans and teammates are betrayed, careers and souls destroyed, for an untrustworthy promise of dirty money" (137-38). One can argue that, like the film

Raging Bull (1980), *Eight Men Out* is not a "sports film." This, of course, calls into question the whole notion of "genre" in film studies, or else suggests that one redefine "sports films."

6. There are many other films that use "home movies" to further plot lines, or to help characters and audience reach resolution. Among them are *Adam's Rib* (1949), in which sparring spouses Tracy and Hepburn reunite while watching home movies; *Guarding Tess* (1994), in which widowed First Lady Tess (Shirley MacLaine) comes to value her bodyguard (Nicholas Cage) while watching a video of her husband's funeral, and *Philadelphia* (1994), which shows us, as the final credits roll, home videos of a young boy whom we recognize and mourn as the younger version of AIDS victim Tom Hanks.

FILMOGRAPHY

Year	Film	Director

Introduction

1939	*Gone with the Wind*	Victor Fleming
1946	*The Yearling*	Clarence Brown
1955	*East of Eden*	Elia Kazan
1965	*The Sound of Music*	Robert Wise
1967	*The Graduate*	Mike Nichols
1970	*Catch 22*	Mike Nichols
1971	*Fiddler on the Roof*	Norman Jewison
1972	*The Godfather*	Francis Coppola
1980	*Fame*	Alan Parker
1982	*An Officer and a Gentleman*	Taylor Hackford
1982	*Tootsie*	Sydney Pollack
1985	*The Color Purple*	Steven Spielberg
1986	*Crimes of the Heart*	Bruce Beresford
1988	*Working Girl*	Mike Nichols
1991	*Billy Bathgate*	Robert Benton
1992	*Leap of Faith*	Richard Pearce

Chapter One: The Rituals of the Godfathers

1909	*A Corner of Wheat*	D. W. Griffith
1972	*The Godfather*	Francis Coppola
1974	*The Godfather Part II*	Francis Coppola
1990	*The Godfather Part III*	Francis Coppola

Chapter Two: The Ritual Occasions of Childhood

1921	*The Kid*	Charles Chaplin
1928	*Our Dancing Daughters*	Harry Beaumont
1935	*Ah, Wilderness*	Clarence Brown
1937	*Stella Dallas*	King Vidor

Filmography

1939	*The Wizard of Oz*	Victor Fleming
1945	*A Tree Grows in Brooklyn*	Elia Kazan
1946	*The Best Years of Our Lives*	William Wyler
1947	*Good News*	Charles Walters
1948	*A Date with Judy*	Richard Thorpe
1950	*All About Eve*	Joseph Mankiewicz
1950	*Our Very Own*	David Miller
1954	*East of Eden*	Elia Kazan
1954	*A Star Is Born*	George Cukor
1954	*The Wild One*	Laslo Benedek
1955	*The Night of the Hunter*	Charles Laughton
1955	*Rebel Without a Cause*	Nicholas Ray
1956	*Carousel*	Henry King
1956	*Giant*	George Stevens
1959	*The Diary of Anne Frank*	George Stevens
1959	*The Four Hundred Blows*	Francois Truffaut
1962	*To Kill a Mockingbird*	Robert Mulligan
1963	*The Courtship of Eddie's Father*	Vincent Minnelli
1964	*Dr. Strangelove*	Stanley Kubrick
1966	*The Blue Max*	John Guillermin
1966	*The Group*	Sidney Lumet
1966	*Who's Afraid of Virgina Woolf?*	Mike Nichols
1967	*Bonnie and Clyde*	Arthur Penn
1967	*The Graduate*	Mike Nichols
1968	*2001: A Space Odyssey*	Stanley Kubrick
1969	*Easy Rider*	Dennis Hopper
1970	*Catch-22*	Mike Nichols
1971	*The Last Picture Show*	Peter Bogdanovich
1973	*The Exorcist*	William Friedkin
1974	*The Great Gatsby*	Jack Clayton
1975	*Smile*	Michael Ritchie
1976	*The Enforcer*	James Fargo
1976	*Taxi Driver*	Martin Scorsese
1977	*Cross of Iron*	Sam Peckinpah
1977	*Star Wars*	George Lucas
1978	*Pretty Baby*	Louis Malle
1979	*The Great Santini*	Lewis Carlino
1979	*I Know Why the Caged Bird Sings*	Fielder Cook
1979	*Kramer vs. Kramer*	Robert Benton
1980	*Ordinary People*	Robert Redford

1980	*Fame*	Alan Parker
1981	*Mommie Dearest*	Frank Perry
1982	*Tootsie*	Sydney Pollack
1983	*Terms of Endearment*	James L. Brooks
1984	*Sixteen Candles*	John Hughes
1985	*Witness*	Peter Weir
1987	*Au Revoir, Les Enfants*	Louis Malle
1987	*Empire of the Sun*	Steven Spielberg
1989	*Crimes and Misdemeanors*	Woody Allen
1989	*Driving Miss Daisy*	Bruce Beresford
1989	*In Country*	Norman Jewison
1989	*Last Exit to Brooklyn*	Uli Edel
1989	*The Music Box*	Costa-Gavras
1989	*Steel Magnolias*	Herbert Ross
1990	*Eating*	Henry Jaglon
1990	*Stella*	John Erman
1991	*Billy Bathgate*	Robert Benton
1991	*City Slickers*	Ron Underwood
1991	*Europa, Europa*	Agnieska Holland
1991	*Once Around*	Lasse Hallstrom
1992	*Radio Flyer*	Richard Donner
1993	*King of the Hill*	Steven Soderbergh
1993	*Made in America*	Richard Benjamin
1993	*This Boy's Life*	Michael Caton-Jones
1993	*What's Eating Gilbert Grape?*	Lasse Hallstrom
1994	*The Client*	Joel Schumacher
1994	*Reality Bites*	Ben Stiller
1994	*With Honors*	Alek Keshishian
1995	*Boys on the Side*	Herbert Ross
1995	*Waiting to Exhale*	Forest Whitaker
1997	*L.A. Confidential*	Curtis Hanson

Chapter Three: Wedding Celebrations

1934	*It Happened One Night*	Frank Capra
1939	*Gone with the Wind*	Victor Fleming
1940	*The Philadelphia Story*	George Cukor
1942	*The Palm Beach Story*	Preston Sturges
1946	*The Best Years of Our Lives*	William Wyler
1946	*The Stranger*	Orson Welles

126 · Filmography

1950	*Father of the Bride*	Vincent Minnelli
1951	*The African Queen*	John Huston
1951	*Royal Wedding*	Stanley Donen
1952	*High Noon*	Fred Zinneman
1955	*Oklahoma!*	Fred Zinneman
1956	*Giant*	George Stevens
1957	*Sayonara*	Joshua Logan
1959	*The Young Philadelphians*	Vincent Sherman
1961	*Bridge to the Sun*	Etienne Perier
1962	*Light in the Piazza*	Guy Green
1965	*The Sound of Music*	Robert Wise
1966	*The Group*	Sidney Lumet
1967	*The Graduate*	Mike Nichols
1969	*Goodbye Columbus*	Larry Peerce
1970	*Lovers and Other Strangers*	Cy Howard
1972	*Cabaret*	Bob Fosse
1972	*The Godfather*	Francis Coppola
1972	*The Heartbreak Kid*	Elaine May
1975	*Cousin, Cousine*	Jean Tacchella
1975	*Nashville*	Robert Altman
1977	*New York, New York*	Martin Scorsese
1978	*Days of Heaven*	Terrence Mallick
1978	*The Deer Hunter*	Michael Cimino
1978	*A Wedding*	Robert Altman
1979	*Rocky II*	Sylvester Stallone
1979	*Quintet*	Robert Altman
1980	*Private Benjamin*	Howard Zieff
1981	*Ragtime*	Milos Forman
1981	*Four Friends*	Arthur Penn
1982	*Best Friends*	Barry Levinson
1985	*The Color Purple*	Steven Spielberg
1985	*Cocoon*	Ron Howard
1985	*Out of Africa*	Sydney Pollack
1985	*Prizzi's Honor*	John Huston
1985	*Twice in a Lifetime*	Bud Yorkin
1987	*Broadcast News*	James L. Brooks
1988	*The Accidental Tourist*	Lawrence Kasdan
1988	*Beaches*	Garry Marshall
1988	*Coming to America*	John Landis
1988	*Mystic Pizza*	Donald Petrie

1988	*Working Girl*	Mike Nichols
1989	*Crimes and Misdemeanors*	Woody Allen
1989	*Sea of Love*	Harold Becker
1989	*Steel Magnolias*	Herbert Ross
1989	*Turner and Hootch*	R. Spottiswoode
1989	*Valmont*	Milos Forman
1989	*When Harry Met Sally*	Rob Reiner
1990	*Come See the Paradise*	Alan Parker
1990	*Cousins*	Joel Schumacher
1990	*True Love*	Nancy Savoca
1991	*Fried Green Tomatoes*	Jon Avnet
1991	*Heaven and Earth*	Oliver Stone
1992	*Mambo Kings*	Arne Glimcher
1992	*Prelude to a Kiss*	Norman Rene
1992	*Unforgiven*	Clint Eastwood
1994	*Four Weddings and a Funeral*	Mike Newell
1994	*Ready to Wear*	Robert Altman
1995	*Mi Familia/My Family*	Gregory Nava

Chapter Four: Wakes, Funerals, and Burials

1909	*A Corner of Wheat*	D. W. Griffith
1911	*Ramona*	D. W. Griffith
1915	*Birth of a Nation*	D. W. Griffith
1928	*The Wind*	Victor Seastrom
1933	*His Double Life*	Arthur Hopkins
1934	*Imitation of Life*	John M. Stahl
1941	*Citizen Kane*	Orson Welles
1943	*Action in the North Atlantic*	Lloyd Bacon
1943	*Holy Matrimony*	John M. Stahl
1944	*Murder, My Sweet*	Edward Dmytryk
1941	*The Maltese Falcon*	John Huston
1948	*Fort Apache*	John Ford
1949	*Battleground*	William Wellman
1949	*Sands of Iwo Jima*	Allan Dwan
1949	*She Wore a Yellow Ribbon*	John Ford
1949	*Three Godfathers*	John Ford
1950	*Rio Grande*	John Ford
1951	*Steel Helmet*	Samuel Fuller
1951	*Westward the Women*	William Wellman

Filmography

1952	*The Bad and the Beautiful*	Vincent Minnelli
1953	*From Here to Eternity*	Fred Zinneman
1955	*Oklahoma!*	Fred Zinneman
1956	*The Searchers*	John Ford
1958	*The Vikings*	Richard Fleischer
1959	*Imitation of Life*	Douglas Sirk
1964	*The Long Ships*	Jack Cardiff
1964	*What a Way to Go!*	J. Lee Thompson
1965	*Doctor Zhivago*	David Lean
1965	*The Loved One*	Tony Richardson
1966	*The Group*	Sidney Lumet
1968	*Bye Bye Braverman*	Sidney Lumet
1969	*Paint Your Wagon*	Joshua Logan
1970	*M*A*S*H*	Robert Altman
1971	*McCabe and Mrs. Miller*	Robert Altman
1972	*Harold and Maude*	Hal Ashby
1972	*Jeremiah Johnson*	Sydney Pollack
1973	*Paper Moon*	Peter Bogdanovich
1978	*The Deer Hunter*	Michael Cimino
1979	*Being There*	Hal Ashby
1980	*Private Benjamin*	Howard Zieff
1981	*Chariots of Fire*	Hugh Hudson
1981	*Excalibur*	John Boorman
1981	*Ragtime*	Milos Forman
1981	*S.O.B.*	Blake Edwards
1983	*The Big Chill*	Lawrence Kadsen
1983	*The Right Stuff*	Philip Kaufman
1985	*The Color Purple*	Steven Spielberg
1986	*Heartburn*	Mike Nichols
1988	*Rain Man*	Barry Levinson
1989	*Valmont*	Milos Forman
1990	*Avalon*	Barry Levinson
1990	*Men Don't Leave*	Paul Brickman
1991	*My Girl*	Howard Zieff
1991	*Only the Lonely*	Chris Columbus
1992	*Passed Away*	Charlie Peters
1992	*Used People*	Beeban Kidron
1995	*Devil in a Blue Dress*	Jonathan Demme
1997	*First Knight*	Jerry Zuker
1997	*Starship Troopers*	Paul Verhoeven

Chapter Five: Luminous Moments in Hollywood Films

1940	*The Philadelphia Story*	George Cukor
1945	*A Tree Grows in Brooklyn*	Elia Kazan
1948	*The Best Years of Our Lives*	William Wyler
1949	*Adam's Rib*	George Cukor
1950	*Our Very Own*	David Miller
1967	*The Graduate*	Mike Nichols
1972	*The Godfather*	Francis Coppola
1972	*Harold and Maude*	Hal Ashby
1973	*American Graffiti*	George Lucas
1974	*The Godfather Part II*	Francis Coppola
1974	*The Longest Yard*	Robert Aldrich
1976	*The Bad News Bears*	Michael Ritchie
1976	*Rocky*	Sylvester Stallone
1978	*The Deer Hunter*	Michael Cimino
1978	*Heaven Can Wait*	Warren Beatty
1979	*Breaking Away*	Peter Yates
1979	*Norma Rae*	Martin Ritt
1980	*Raging Bull*	Martin Scorsese
1981	*Chariots of Fire*	Hugh Hudson
1983	*All the Right Moves*	Michael Chapman
1984	*The Karate Kid*	John Avildsen
1984	*The Natural*	Barry Levinson
1984	*Places in the Heart*	Robert Benton
1984	*Sixteen Candles*	John Hughes
1985	*The Color Purple*	Steven Spielberg
1985	*St. Elmo's Fire*	Joel Schumacher
1985	*Vision Quest*	Harold Becker
1986	*Hoosiers*	David Anspaugh
1988	*Bull Durham*	Ron Shelton
1988	*Cinema Paradiso*	G. Tornatore
1988	*Eight Men Out*	John Sayles
1989	*Field of Dreams*	Phil Robinson
1989	*Major League*	David S. Ward
1990	*The Godfather Part III*	Francis Coppola
1990	*Men Don't Leave*	Paul Brickman
1990	*Postcards from the Edge*	Mike Nichols
1991	*Fried Green Tomatoes*	John Avnet
1991	*Once Around*	Lasse Hallstrom
1992	*A League of Their Own*	Penny Marshall

1993	*Philadelphia*	Jonathan Demme
1993	*Rudy*	David Anspaugh
1994	*The Air Up There*	Paul Michael Glazer
1994	*Guarding Tess*	Hugh Wilson
1994	*Reality Bites*	Ben Stiller
1995	*Higher Learning*	John Singleton

WORKS CITED

Abrahams, Roger D. "The Language of Festivals: Celebrating the Economy." *Celebration: Studies in Festivity and Ritual.* Ed. Victor Turner. Washington, D.C.: Smithsonian, 1982. 161-77.

Adair, Gilbert. *Vietnam on Film: From "The Green Berets" to "Apocalypse Now."* New York: Proteus, 1981.

Alpert, Hollis. "*The Graduate* Makes Out." *The Movies: An American Idiom: Readings in the Social History of the American Motion Picture.* Ed. Arthur F. McClure. Cranbury, NJ: Associated UP, 1971.

Ardolino, Frank. "Ceremonies of Innocence and Experience in *Bull Durham, Field of Dreams,* and *Eight Men Out.*" *Journal of Popular Film & Television* 18 (Summer 1990): 43-51.

Auster, Albert, and Leonard Quart. *How the War Was Remembered: Hollywood and Vietnam.* New York: Praeger, 1988.

Bergan, Ronald. *Sports in the Movies.* New York: Proteus, 1982.

Boyd, David. "*The Deer Hunter:* The Hero and the Tradition." *Australian Journal of American Studies* 1 (1980): 41-45.

Brode, Douglas. *The Films of the Fifties.* Secaucus, NJ: Citadel P, 1976.

Browne, Ray B., ed. *Rituals and Ceremonies in Popular Culture.* Bowling Green, OH: Bowling Green State University Popular Press, 1980.

Byars, Jackie. *All That Hollywood Allows: Re-reading Gender in 1950s Melodrama.* Chapel Hill: U of North Carolina P, 1991.

Cagin, Seth, and Philip Dray. *Hollywood Films of the Seventies: Sex, Drugs, Violence, Rock'n'Roll & Politics.* New York: Harper, 1984.

Campbell, Joseph. *The Hero with a Thousand Faces.* Princeton: Princeton UP, 1949.

Cavell, Stanley. *Pursuits of Happiness: The Hollywood Comedy of Remarriage.* Cambridge: Harvard UP, 1981.

Cook, David A. *A History of Narrative Film.* 2nd ed. New York: Norton, 1990.
Cripps, Thomas R. *Black Film as Genre.* Bloomington: Indiana UP, 1978.
——. "The Death of Rastus: Negroes in American Films Since 1945." *The Movies: An American Idiom: Readings in the Social History of the American Motion Picture.* Ed. Arthur F. McClure. Cranbury, NJ: Associated UP, 1971.
——. *Slow Fade to Black: The Negro in American Film, 1900-1942.* New York: Oxford UP, 1977.
Denby, David. *America in the Dark: Hollywood and the Gift of Unreality.* New York: Morrow, 1977.
Doane, Mary Ann. *The Desire to Desire: The Woman's Film of the 1940s.* Bloomington: Indiana UP, 1987.
Doane, Mary Ann, Patricia Mellencamp, and Linda Williams, eds. *Revision.* Frederick, MD: U Publications of America, 1984.
Driver, Thomas F. *The Magic of Ritual.* San Francisco: Harper, 1991.
Erikson, Eric H. *Toys and Reasons: Stages in the Ritualization of Experience.* New York: Norton, 1977.
Erens, Patricia. *The Jew in American Cinema.* Bloomington: Indiana UP, 1984.
Freydberg, Elizabeth Hadley. "Women of Color: No Joy in the Seduction of Images." *Multiple Voices in Feminist Film Criticism,* Ed. Diane Carson, Linda Dittmar, and Janice R. Welsch. Minneapolis: U of Minnesota P, 1994. 468-80.
Friedman, Lester, ed. *Unspeakable Images: Ethnicity and the American Cinema.* Urbana: U of Illinois P, 1991.
Gibson-Hudson, Gloria. "Aspects of Black Feminist Cultural Ideology in Films by Black Women Independent Artists *Multiple Voices in Feminist Film Criticism.* Ed. Diane Carson, Linda Dittmar, and Janice R. Welsch. Minneapolis: U of Minnesota P, 1994. 365-79.
Good, Howard. "Extra Innings: Bats, Balls and Gloves in Baseball Films of the 1980s." *Beyond the Stars; Studies in American Popular Film.* Vol. 3. Ed. Paul Loukides and Linda K. Fuller. Bowling Green, OH: Bowling Green State University Popular Press, 1993. 134-48.

Griffith, David Wark. *The Man Who Invented Hollywood: The Autobiography of D. W. Griffith.* Ed. James Hart. Louisville, KY: Touchstone, 1972.
Grimes, Ronald L. "The Lifeblood of Public Ritual: Fiestas and Public Exploration Projects." *Celebration: Studies in Festivity and Ritual.* Ed. Victor Turner. Washington, D.C.: Smithsonian, 1982. 272-83.
Harvey, James. *Romantic Comedy in Hollywood from Lubitsch to Sturges.* New York: Knopf, 1987.
Haskell, Molly. *From Reverence to Rape: The Treatment of Women in the Movies.* Chicago: U of Chicago P, 1987.
Hellman, John. *American Myth and the Legacy of Vietnam.* New York: Columbia UP, 1986.
Hess, John. "*Godfather II*: A Deal Coppola Couldn't Refuse." *Movies and Methods.* Ed. Bill Nichols. Berkeley: U of California P, 1976.
Heung, Marina. "'What's the Matter with Sara Jane?': Daughters and Mothers in Douglas Sirk's *Imitation of Life*." *Cinema Journal* 26.3 (Spring 1987): 21-43.
hooks, bell. "A Call for Militant Resistance." *Multiple Voices in Feminist Film Criticism.* Ed. Diane Carson, Linda Dittmar, and Janice R. Welsch. Minneapolis: U of Minnesota P, 1994. 358-64.
Jacobs, Lewis. "World War II and the American Film." *Cinema Journal* 7.1 (Winter 1967-68): 1-21.
Johnson, Robert K. *Francis Ford Coppola.* Boston: Hall, 1977.
Kaplan, E. Ann, ed. *Women in Film Noir.* London: British Film Institute, 1980.
Kolker, Robert Phillip. *A Cinema of Loneliness: Penn, Kubrick, Coppola, Scorsese, Altman.* New York: Oxford UP, 1980.
Lawson, Thomas, and Robert N. McCauley. *Rethinking Religion: Connecting Cognition and Culture.* New York: Cambridge UP, 1990.
Loukides, Paul. "The Celebration of Family Plot: Episodes and Affirmations." *Beyond the Stars; Studies in American Popular Film.* Vol. II. Ed. Paul Loukides and Linda K. Fuller. Bowling Green, OH: Bowling Green State University Popular Press, 1991. 91-99.
MacAloon, John J. "Sociation and Sociability in Political Celebrations." *Celebration: Studies in Festivity and Ritual.* Ed. Victor Turner. Washington, D.C.: Smithsonian, 1982. 255-71.

Maio, Kathi. *Feminist in the Dark: Reviewing the Movies.* Freedom, CA: Crossing P, 1988.

Marsden, Michael T. "Western Films: America's Secularized Religion." *Movies as Artifacts: Cultural Criticism of Popular Film.* Ed. Michael T. Marsden, John G. Nachbar, and Sam L. Grogg, Jr. Chicago: Nelson-Hall, 1982, 105-14.

Myerhoff, Barbara. "Rites of Passage: Process and Paradox." *Celebration: Studies in Festivity and Ritual.* Ed. Victor Turner. Washington, D.C.: Smithsonian, 1982, 109-35.

Nachbar, John, ed. *Focus on the Western.* Englewood Cliffs, NJ: Prentice-Hall, 1974.

Nichols, Bill, ed. *Movies and Methods.* Berkeley: U of California P, 1976.

Noverr, Douglas A. "The Coach and the Athlete in Football Sports Films." *Beyond the Stars; Studies in American Popular Film.* Vol. 1. Ed. Paul Loukides and Linda K. Fuller. Bowling Green, OH: Bowling Green State U Popular P, 1990. 120-29.

Parish, James Robert, and Michael R. Pitts. *The Great Detective Pictures.* New York: Scarecrow, 1990.

Ray, Robert B. *A Certain Tendency of the Hollywood Cinema, 1930-1980.* Princeton: Princeton UP, 1985.

Sayre, Nora. "Winning the Weepstakes: The Problems of American Sports Movies." *Film Genre: Theory and Criticism.* Ed. Grant Barryk. Metuchen, NJ: Scarecrow, 1977. 182-94.

Selby, Spencer. *Dark City: The Film Noir.* New York: St. James, 1984.

Shadoian, Jack. *Dreams and Dead Ends: The American Gangster/Crime Film.* Cambridge, MA: MIT P, 1977.

Slotkin, Richard. "Prologue to a Study of Myth and Genre in American Movies." *Prospects: The Annual of American Cultural Studies.* Vol. 9. Ed. Jack Salzman. Cambridge: Cambridge UP, 1984.

Sodowsky, Barbara, Roland Sodowsky, and Stephen Witte. "The Epic World of *American Graffiti.*" *Movies As Artifacts: Cultural Criticism of Popular Film.* Ed Michael T. Marsden, John G. Nachbar, and Sam L. Grogg, Jr. Chicago: Nelson-Hall, 1982. 217-22.

Stubbs, Frances, and Elizabeth Hadley Freydberg. "Black Women in American Films: A Thematic Approach." *Multiple Voices in Fem-*

inist Film Criticism. Ed. Diane Carson, Linda Dittmar, and Janice R. Welsch. Minneapolis: U of Minnesota P, 1994. 481-91.

Suid, Lawrence T. *Guts and Glory: Great American War Movies.* Reading, MA: Addison-Wesley, 1978.

Thomson, David. "The Lives of Supporting Players." *Film Commentary* (Nov.-Dec. 1989): 32-34.

———. *Overexposures: The Crisis in American Filmmaking.* New York: Morrow, 1981.

Turner, Victor. *Dramas, Fields, and Metaphors: Symbolic Action in Human Society.* Ithaca: Cornell UP, 1974.

———. *From Ritual to Theatre: The Human Seriousness of Play.* New York: Performing Arts Journal Publications, 1982.

———. *The Ritual Process: Structure and Anti-Structure.* Chicago: Aldine, 1969.

Williams, Linda. "'Something Else Besides a Mother': *Stella Dallas* and the Maternal Melodrama." *Cinema Journal* 24.1 (Fall 1984): 2-27.

Williams, Martin. *Griffith: First Artist of the Movies.* New York: Oxford UP, 1980.

Wilson, James C. *Vietnam in Prose and Film.* Jefferson, MO: McFarland, 1982.

Winokur, Mark. "Black Is White/White Is Black: 'Passing' as a Strategy of Racial Compatibility in Contemporary Hollywood Comedy." *Unspeakable Images: Ethnicity and the American Cinema.* Ed. Lester D. Friedman. Urbana: U of Illinois P, 1991. 190-211.

Wood, Rubin. *Hollywood from Vietnam to Reagan.* New York: Columbia UP, 1986.

Yates, John. "*Godfather* Saga: The Death of a Family." *Movies as Artifacts: Cultural Criticism of Popular Film.*" Ed. Michael T. Marsden, John G. Nachbar, and Sam L. Grogg, Jr. Chicago: Nelson-Hall, 1982. 198-203.

INDEX

Awards ceremony scenes,
  All About Eve, 117n
  Best Years of Our Lives, 116n
  Blue Max, 116n
  Catch 22, 116n
  Cross of Iron, 116n
  Enforcer, 117n
  King of the Hill, 38-39
  L.A. Confidential, 117n
  Smile, 117n
  A Star Is Born (1954), 116n
  Star Wars, 116n

Baptisms,
  Billy Bathgate, 8
  Color Purple, 8
  Crimes and Misdemeanors, 29
  Godfather, 8, 15-17
  Last Exit to Brooklyn, 29, 41-42
  Leap of Faith, 8
  Once Around, 29
Birthday parties, adult,
  Boys on the Side, 116n
  City Slickers, 116n
  Courtship of Eddie's Father, 116n
  Crimes of the Heart, 7, 109
  Driving Miss Daisy, 116n
  East of Eden, 31-32
  Eating, 116n
  Godfather, 11
  Godfather II, 19, 86-88
  Great Gatsby, 116n
  Music Box, 116n
  Terms of Endearment, 116n
  Tootsie, 7, 116n
  Waiting to Exhale, 116n
Birthday parties, juvenile,
  Fame, 7, 40
  Giant, 32-33, 41
  Graduate, 7, 33-35, 102
  Great Santini, 36
  Mommie Dearest, 36
  Our Very Own, 29, 102
  Sixteen Candles, 36, 90
  Steel Magnolias, 40
  Stella Dallas, 115n
  What's Eating Gilbert Grape?, 36
  Who's Afraid of Virginia Woolf? 33

Coming of age movies,
  Au Revoir, Les Enfants, 116n
  Client, 116n
  Diary of Anne Frank, 116n
  East of Eden, 7, 31-32

137

Europa, Europa, 116n
Empire of the Sun, 116n
Exorcist, 116n
Four Hundred Blows, 116n
King of the Hill, 37-39
Kramer v. Kramer, 36
Night of the Hunter, 116n
Ordinary People, 36
Pretty Baby, 36
Radio Flyer, 116n
Rebel without a Cause, 31
Taxi Driver, 36
This Boy's Life, 116n
To Kill a Mockingbird, 116n
Tree Grows in Brooklyn, 27-28, 30, 41, 90, 102, 115n
Wild One, 31
Witness, 116n

First Communion,
  Godfather II, 17-18
Funerals,
  Action in the North Atlantic, 70
  Avalon, 84
  Bad and the Beautiful, 74
  Battleground, 70
  Being There, 77
  Big Chill, 74-75, 78, 80
  Bye Bye, Braverman, 74
  Catch-22, 7
  Chariots of Fire, 73
  Citizen Kane, 83
  Color Purple, 75
  Deer Hunter, 73, 84
  Devil in a Blue Dress, 73
  Doctor Zhivago, 75
  Fort Apache, 68
  Four Weddings and a Funeral, 109-10
  From Here to Eternity, 84
  Godfather, 15, 24
  Godfather II, 17, 19-20
  Group, 73, 84
  Guarding Tess, 122n
  Harold and Maude, 75-76, 77, 85
  His Double Life, 77
  Holy Matrimony, 77
  Imitation of Life (1934), 80, 120n
  Imitation of Life (1959), 80-82, 120n
  Jeremiah Johnson, 68
  Loved One, 75-76
  Maltese Falcon, 73
  *M*A*S*H*, 77
  Men Don't Leave, 83
  Murder, My Sweet, 73
  My Girl, 78-79, 80
  Oklahoma! 82
  Only the Lonely, 77
  Out of Africa, 109, 110
  Paint Your Wagon, 82
  Paper Moon, 75
  Passed Away, 77
  Private Benjamin, 77
  Ragtime, 83
  Rain Man, 75
  Right Stuff, 71-73
  Rio Grande, 68
  Sands of Iwo Jima, 70-71
  Searchers, 68-69, 70, 83
  She Wore a Yellow Ribbon, 68

Index · 139

Steel Helmet, 70
Three Godfathers, 68-69, 70
Tree Grows in Brooklyn, 31
Used People, 77
Westward the Women, 68
What a Way to Go! 77
Wind, 66-67, 68
Yearling, 7
Funerals, comedy,
   Being There, 77
   Bye Bye, Braverman, 74
   Big Chill, 74,75, 78, 80
   Four Weddings and a Funeral, 109-10
   Harold and Maude, 75-76, 77, 85
   His Double Life, 77
   Holy Matrimony, 77
   Loved One, 75-76
   M*A*S*H, 77
   Men Don't Leave, 83
   Only the Lonely, 77
   Paper Moon, 75
   Passed Away, 77
   Used People, 77
   What a Way to Go! 77
Funerals, crime drama,
   Devil in a Blue Dress, 73
   Maltese Falcon, 73
   Murder, My Sweet, 73
Funerals, military,
   Action in the North Atlantic, 70
   Battleground, 70
   Catch-22, 7
   Deer Hunter, 73, 84
   From Here to Eternity, 84

   M*A*S*H, 77
   Right Stuff, 71-73
   Sands of Iwo Jima, 70-71
   Steel Helmet, 70
Funerals, western,
   Fort Apache, 68
   Jeremiah Johnson, 68
   Rio Grande, 68
   Searchers, 68-69, 70, 83
   She Wore a Yellow Ribbon, 68
   Three Godfathers, 68-69, 70
   Westward the Women, 68
   Wind, 66-67, 68

Graduation ceremonies,
   Ah, Wilderness! 26, 39
   Fame, 37
   Graduate, 33-35, 39, 40
   Group, 37
   I Know Why the Caged Bird Sings, 40
   In Country, 37, 40
   King of the Hill, 37-39
   Last Picture Show, 37, 39
   Made in America, 37
   Officer and a Gentleman, 8
   Our Very Own, 29-30
   Reality Bites, 37, 40, 41
   St. Elmo's Fire, 85
   Tree Grows in Brooklyn, 28, 30, 37, 115n
   With Honors, 37

Implied ritual scenes (off screen),
   Godfather, 111
   Gone with the Wind, 111
   Graduate, 33, 110

140 · Index

Love Story, 111
Ordinary People, 111-12
Terms of Endearment, 111
Top Gun, 111
War of the Roses, 111
When Harry Met Sally, 111

"Luminous" scenes in movies,
  Adam's Rib, 122n
  American Graffiti, 91-92
  Best Years of Our Lives, 90
  Cinema Paradiso, 105
  Color Purple, 91
  Fried Green Tomatoes, 91
  Godfather, 88-89, 90, 106
  Godfather II, 89
  Godfather III, 89
  Guarding Tess, 122n
  Men Don't Leave, 91
  Natural, 102
  Norma Rae, 91
  Once Around, 105-06
  Philadelphia, 122n
  Philadelphia Story, 92
  Places in the Heart, 92
  Postcards from the Edge, 90, 91

Sports films and ritual,
  Air Up There, 95, 98, 99, 100
  All the Right Moves, 99
  Bad News Bears, 102
  Breaking Away, 93, 95, 98, 99, 100, 102
  Bull Durham, 101
  Chariots of Fire, 97
  Eight Men Out, 121-22n

  Field of Dreams, 98, 99, 101, 103
  Heaven Can Wait, 93
  Higher Learning, 102
  Hoosiers, 98, 100, 102
  Karate Kid, 102
  League of Their Own, 96, 97, 98, 99, 101
  Longest Yard, 95, 98, 99
  Major League, 97-98, 99
  Natural, 98, 99, 101, 102
  Raging Bull, 121-22n
  Rocky, 98, 103
  Rudy, 94, 98
  Vision Quest, 94, 102

Weddings,
  Accidental Tourist, 59
  African Queen, 44
  Beaches, 118n
  Best Friends, 118n
  Best Years of Our Lives, ix, 44, 60
  Bride of Frankenstein, 44
  Bridge to the Sun, 61
  Broadcast News, 118n
  Cabaret, 60
  Color Purple, 61
  Come See the Paradise, 61
  Coming to America, 118n
  Cocoon, 119n
  Cousin, Cousine, 118n
  Cousins, 118n
  Crimes and Misdemeanors, 118n
  Days of Heaven, 44, 60
  Deer Hunter, 56-58, 85, 118n

Index

Father of the Bride, 43-44, 45-46, 60, 61, 62, 63
Fiddler on the Roof, 7, 109
Four Friends, 119n
Four Weddings and a Funeral, 110, 119n
Fried Green Tomatoes, 44
Giant, 59
Godfather, iv, xii, 13-15, 53-56, 58, 118n
Godfather III, 21
Gone with the Wind, 7, 111
Goodbye Columbus, 47-50, 118n
Graduate, 46-47, 50, 117n
Group, 59
Heartbreak Kid, 48-50, 118n
Heaven and Earth, 61
High Noon, 44
It Happened One Night, 46, 50, 51
Last Exit to Brooklyn, 42
Light in the Piazza, 118n
Lovers and Other Strangers, 44
Mambo Kings, 61
Mi Familia, 61
Mystic Pizza, 50, 51, 52-53
New York, New York, 44
Oklahoma! 44, 119n
Out of Africa, 44
Palm Beach Story, 50, 51
Philadelphia Story, 46
Prelude to a Kiss, 118n
Private Benjamin, ix, 44, 50, 51-52
Prizzi's Honor, 86

Ragtime, 63
Rocky II, 118n
Royal Wedding, 44
Sayonara, 44, 61, 119n
Sound of Music, 7, 44
Steel Magnolias, 118n
Stranger, 118n
True Love, 118n
Turner and Hootch, 118n
Twice in a Lifetime, 118n
Unforgiven, 60
Valmont, 118n
Wedding, 62-63, 119n
When Harry Met Sally, 111, 118n
Working Girl, 7, 59
Young Philadelphians, 44
Weddings, doomed,
  Cabaret, 60
  Days of Heaven, 44, 60
  Deer Hunter, 56-58, 85, 118n
  Four Friends, 119n
  Godfather, iv, xii, 13-15, 53-56, 58, 118n
  Graduate, 46-47, 50, 117n
  Group, 59
  Heartbreak Kid, 48-50, 118n
  Mi Familia, 61
  Oklahoma! 44, 119n
  Private Benjamin, ix, 44, 50, 51-52
  Sayonara, 44, 61, 119n
  Unforgiven, 60
  Wedding, 62-63, 119n
Weddings, ethnic,
  Color Purple, 61
  Come See the Paradise, 61

Goodbye Columbus, 47-50, 118n
Heartbreak Kid, 48-50, 118n
Heaven and Earth, 61
Mambo Kings, 61
Mi Familia, 61
Mystic Pizza, 50, 51, 52-53
Sayonara, 44, 61, 119n
Unforgiven, 60

Weddings, multiple,
Four Weddings and a Funeral, 109, 110, 119n
Godfather, iv, xii, 13-15, 53-56, 58, 118n
Heartbreak Kid, 48-50, 118n
Mystic Pizza, 50, 51, 52-53
Palm Beach Story, 50, 51
Private Benjamin, ix, 44, 50, 51-52
Working Girl, 7, 59